NEW MEXICO

ART OF THE STATE

ART OF THE STATE

NEW MEXICO

The Spirit of America

Text by Cynthia Bix

Harry N. Abrams, Inc., Publishers

NEW YORK

This book was prepared for publication at
Walking Stick Press, San Francisco

Project staff:
 Series Designer: Linda Herman
 Series Editor: Diana Landau

For Harry N. Abrams, Inc.:
 Series Editor: Ruth A. Peltason

Page 1: *Hopi Snake Priest (Beaded Portrait)* by Marcus Amerman,
 after a photograph by Edward S. Curtis, 1986. *American Indian
 Contemporary Arts, San Francisco*

Page 2: *Tree of Life* by George Lopez, c. 1950. *Museum of International
 Folk Art, Santa Fe. Photo Michel Monteaux*

Library of Congress Cataloging-in-Publication Data

Bix, Cynthia Overbeck.
 New Mexico : the spirit of America state by state / by Cynthia Bix
  p. cm. — (Art of the state)
 ISBN 0–8109–5553–9 (hc)
 1. New Mexico—Civilization–Pictorial works. I. Title.
 II. Series.
F797.B59 1998
978.9—dc21   97–12019

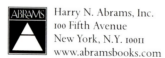
Harry N. Abrams, Inc.
100 Fifth Avenue
New York, N.Y. 10011
www.abramsbooks.com

Mural of St. Joseph and child by Jack Good, on the wall of a Santa Fe home, 1985. The image replicates part of a wood *retablo* in the Santuario de Chimayo. *Photo Jack Parsons*

CONTENTS

"For a greatness of beauty I have never experienced anything like New Mexico....What splendor!"

D. H. Lawrence, "New Mexico," 1931

New Mexico's nickname, "Land of Enchantment," is well chosen, for this land has enchanted its visitors and inhabitants for centuries. The New Mexico experience, as rich and highly seasoned as its famed cuisine, is compounded of a thousand elements that feed the senses and stir the soul—the sharp, geometric patterns of sun and shadow on canyon rock, the vast silence of the desert simmering in the noon heat, the texture of an old adobe wall. Add to these the coyote's song, the aroma of piñon smoke, and fiery color of a chile ristra, and you begin to make a picture of this alluring state.

The first thing that strikes the beholder is New Mexico's extraordinary natural setting. Whether one experiences it as austere and vaguely unsettling or splendid and exalting, this is a place of dramatic natural beauty, whose soaring rock formations, broad mesas, pine mountains, desert expanses, and dazzling skies have inspired generations of artists and adventurers.

The human story of New Mexico has been aptly called a "pageant of three peoples." The first New Mexicans were the Native Americans—the ancient Pueblo people. Theirs was a settled way of life based on agriculture and the rhythms of nature. These remarkable people built great "cities in the sand" centuries ago, and the vigorous culture of their descendants survives today.

In the sixteenth century came the Spanish, up from Mexico along the Camino Real, or King's Road—the great highway that stretched from

Chama Running Red by John Sloan, 1927. *The Anschutz Collection*

Chihuahua to Santa Fe. They brought to the land their lively language and ways, and transformed it into a patchwork of haciendas and vast cattle and sheep ranchos. Finally, with the opening of the Santa Fe Trail, Anglo-Americans from the East poured in, bringing with them the railroad, the cattle drive, the oil well, and the towns and cities that naturally followed. A still later "invasion"—the steady stream of artists attracted to the beauties of Santa Fe and Taos at the turn of the century—has contributed yet another dimension of color and character to the state.

While New Mexico's ethnic communities have sometimes clashed, they have usually managed to coexist in a rare harmony of cultures. Traditionally, what has bound together Native Americans, Hispanics, and Anglos is a common response to the demands of the land. They have shared the all-important quest for water, the shaping of the clay soil into adobe for building in a land with few trees, the cultivation of the few crops and livestock that thrive here. Religion, too, has played a central role in New Mexican life, deeply underlying both Pueblo and Hispanic cultures. The Native spiritual traditions contrast strongly with the fervent Roman Catholicism of the Hispanics, but gradually they have blended, with saints or spirits from both cultures bringing passion and pageantry to celebrations throughout the year.

New Mexicans also find common ground in the impulse to make art in response to the world they inhabit. The result is a great wellspring of fine art, architecture, folk art, crafts, and lively arts unique to the region. Much of it follows the "pure" forms of a distinct tradition: for example, the Native Americans' graceful pottery and jewelry; the expressive painted *bultos*, or saint figures, carved by Hispanic *santeros*, and the organic forms of adobe dwellings. Other works are an expression of synthesis: painters, sculptors, and craftspeople combining old with new, Native American and Spanish with elements of modernism, to create highly personal visions. In design, the popular "Santa Fe style" has introduced the New Mexico aesthetic to interiors around the world. Even in the art of cookery, traditional ingredients like chiles and corn are given a contemporary twist, with delightful results.

In all ways, New Mexico is a fascinating mix of the old and the new, the traditional and the avant-garde. It's a place for tourists and ranchers, artists

Navajo rug depicting a trading post scene, woven by Laura and Loretta Nez, grandmother and granddaughter, 1993. *Cristof's Santa Fe. Photo Jerry Jacka*

and entrepreneurs, rodeo riders and low-riders. A place where Pueblo corn dances and Catholic saint's days are still rituals of spring, where weathered Spanish *casas* and ancient Pueblo cities doze in the sun, while on the White Sands near Alamagordo missiles are tested. But many feel that the spirit of New Mexico's land and people finds its most vivid and unifying expression through the arts—in painting and pottery, in literature and dance, in the song of the cowboy and in Spanish *canciones*. No matter where they come from, New Mexico's artists have been moved by their surroundings to create works that express the special qualities of life in this enchanted land. ✦

NEW MEXICO

"Land of Enchantment"
47th State

Date of Statehood
JANUARY 6, 1912

Capital
SANTA FE

Bird
ROADRUNNER

Flower
YUCCA

Tree
PIÑON PINE

Stone
TURQUOISE

Animal
BLACK BEAR

Vegetables
CHILE PEPPER, BEANS

For a lively cameo portrait of New Mexico, one need only look to the emblems chosen by its citizens to represent their state. The official salute to New Mexico's flag, which speaks of "perfect friendship among united cultures," sets the tone for a union of Native American, Hispanic, and Anglo-American elements. On the state seal, the great American bald eagle enfolds in its wings

Yucca and roadrunner

a Mexican brown eagle clasping snake and cactus—a symbol very like that of the Mexican Republic, from which so many settlers came. Completing the trio, the state flag features a brilliantly colored Zia symbol from a Pueblo Indian design. The state's striking natural terrain is celebrated in its symbols, too. From the piñon, whose logs send aromatic smoke up thousands of

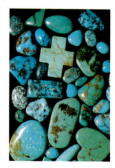

"Crescit eundo" (It grows as it goes)

State motto

chimneys, to the dramatic yucca plant, to the chiles and frijoles that define New Mexican cuisine, the state's official flora are hardy and distinctive. And its official animals, from the speedy roadrunner to the black bear (the model for Smokey himself), reflect the land's natural diversity. ✦

Opposite: **Carved and polished turquoise.** *Historic Old Town Turquoise Museum, Albuquerque. Photo Richard T. Nowitz. Above:* **Piñon pine** *(Pinus edulis), drawing by Mary Beath Illustration Design.*

"O, Fair New Mexico"

Under sky of azure, where balmy breezes blow;
Kissed by the golden sunshine, our native state,
   New Mexico.
Home of the Montezuma, with fiery heart aglow,
State of the deeds historic, Hail to New Mexico.

O, fair New Mexico, we love, we love you so,
Our hearts with pride o'erflow,
No matter where we go,
O, fair New Mexico, we love, we love you so,
The grandest state to know, New Mexico.

Words and music by Elizabeth Garrett
(daughter of Sheriff Pat Garrett), 1915

Bizcochitos

Brought to New Mexico by Spanish settlers, the bizcochito is a small, anise-flavored cookie usually made for special celebrations. Its adoption in 1989 made New Mexico the first state to have an official cookie.

1 ½ cups sugar
1 cup unsalted butter
1 ½ cups all-purpose flour
1 ½ teaspoons anise seed
1 teaspoon baking powder
2 eggs
1 teaspoon brandy
½ teaspoon vanilla
Granulated sugar and cinnamon

Cream together sugar and butter just until well mixed. Sift together flour, anise, and baking powder, stir them into the sugar and butter, then gently stir in eggs, brandy, and vanilla to make a smooth dough. Chill for several hours. Preheat oven to 375°F. Roll dough out to ¼ inch thick on a lightly floured board. Cut with cookie cutter, liberally sprinkle with sugar and cinnamon, and place cookies on a baking sheet lined with parchment paper. Bake about 10 minutes or until lightly browned.

Adapted from John Sedlar's recipe in Modern Southwest Cuisine, *1986*

"ACTUALLY, OF COURSE, TEXAS IS NO BIGGER THAN NEW Mexico. It only appears bigger because it is spread out so much thinner. The mean average thickness of New Mexico from sunshine to sea level is 5,600 feet.... Mashed down and rolled out to the same thickness as Texas, New Mexico would reach all the way from Yalta to the Atlantic Charter with enough lapover to flap in the Texas wind...."

Cowboy poet S. Omar Barker

Above: The Rio Grande cutthroat trout, *Oncorhynchus clarki virginalis,* is New Mexico's state fish. Watercolor by James Prosek, 1996. *Left:* New Mexico's State Capitol, in Santa Fe, was designed by W. C. Kruger in the Territorial Style, a blend of Greek Revival and Pueblo adobe. Locally known as the Round House, it was dedicated in 1966. *Photo Herb Lotz*

The Multicultural State

New Mexico's state flag and license plate bear an ancient sun symbol design adapted from a Zia pueblo water jar, and this emblem of the state's multicultural heritage is noted in the official "salute to the flag":

U.S. postage stamp issued in 1962 in honor of New Mexico's semi-centennial depicts Shiprock, a dramatic landform sacred to the Navajo and visible for many miles distant.

Saludo la bandera del estado de Nuevo Méjico, el símbolo Zia de amistad perfecta, entre culturas unidas.

I salute the flag of New Mexico and the Zia symbol of perfect friendship among united cultures.

Above: 1935 New Mexico road map with Zia symbol. *Courtesy Michael Wallis. Right:* The state fossil is the *Coelophysis* dinosaur, a six-foot carnivore from the Triassic Period, discovered near Ghost Ranch in 1947. *New Mexico Museum of Natural History and Science*

c. 800–1300 A.D. "Golden Age" of Anasazi culture.

1539 Fray Marcos de Niza discovers the "Seven Cities" of Cibola (Zuni Pueblo); takes possession of New Mexico region for Spain.

1540–42 Francisco Vásquez de Coronado's expedition of conquest.

1590–91 First (unauthorized) attempt to colonize New Mexico.

1598 Don Juan de Oñate establishes first Spanish settlement and capital at San Juan Pueblo. First church built there.

1599 Battle of Acoma; Spanish victory.

1610 Santa Fe becomes capital; Palace of the Governors built.

1617 Eleven mission churches in New Mexico. White population, 48 men.

1680 Pueblo Revolt led by the Indian Popé ends Spanish rule temporarily.

1692 Reconquest by Don Diego de Vargas; Indians yield peacefully.

1696 Final Pueblo rebellion and defeat.

1706 Albuquerque founded.

1712 First fiesta season proclaimed in Santa Fe on September 16.

1790 Population (Native and Spanish), 30,953.

1792 Pedro Vial blazes trail from Santa Fe to St. Louis; first complete journey across eventual Santa Fe Trail.

1803 U.S. acquires Louisiana Territory; balance of power in North America shifts.

1821 Mexico declares independence from Spain; New Mexico becomes a province.

1822 William Becknell brings first wagons from the East to Santa Fe.

1834 First newspaper, *La Crepúsculo de la Libertad,* published in Santa Fe.

1841 Texas invasion of New Mexico thwarted by Governor Manual Armijo.

1846 U.S. declares war on Mexico. General Kearny occupies Santa Fe peacefully.

1848 Treaty of Guadalupe Hidalgo; Mexico formally cedes all claims on New Mexico and upper California.

1849 Regular stage line established between Santa Fe and Independence, Mo.

1850 New Mexico becomes a U.S. territory. Population, 61,547.

1853   Gadsden Purchase; U.S. acquires southern New Mexico. Kit Carson becomes an Indian agent in the territory.

1869–86   Archbishop Lamy directs building of St. Francis Cathedral in Santa Fe.

1876–78   Lincoln County War between rival cattlemen and political factions.

1879   First passenger train comes to New Mexico. Frank Hamilton Cushing, patron of Pueblo culture, arrives at Zuni Pueblo.

1880   John K. Hilliers photographs New Mexico for Bureau of American Ethnology.

1881   Billy the Kid shot by Sheriff Pat Garrett.

1883   Artist Joseph Henry Sharp first visits New Mexico.

1886   Apache chief Geronimo surrenders in Mexico.

1891   Charles Lummis's *Land of Poco Tiempo* appears in *Scribner's*.

1898   New Mexico provides 340 troops to Teddy Roosevelt's Rough Riders in Spanish-American War.

1900   New capitol dedicated in Santa Fe.

1907   Palace of the Governors becomes Museum of New Mexico.

1912   New Mexico becomes 47th state.

1916   Pancho Villa raids border town of Columbus, kills U.S. citizens. First Taos Society of Artists traveling exhibition.

1918   Maria and Julian Martinez make first black-on-black pottery.

1919   Santa Fe Fiesta revived.

1920   Spanish Colonial Arts Society founded. Drought and depression through 1923. Population, 360,350.

1923–24   Oil found on Navajo Reservation.

1924   Mary Austin settles in Santa Fe.

1927   Willa Cather's *Death Comes for the Archbishop* published.

1929   Georgia O'Keeffe first visits the state.

1933–43   Federal WPA projects in New Mexico.

1945   World's first atomic explosion at Trinity Site.

1948   New Mexico Native Americans win suffrage.

1956   Santa Fe Opera established.

1970   Congress establishes sacred Blue Lake area as land trust for sole use by people of Taos Pueblo.

1997   50th anniversary of famed UFO "landing" in Roswell.

LAND OF CONTRASTS

The Rio Grande River, flowing through Upper Taos Box Canyon. This great Southwest river carries life-giving mountain snowmelt down out

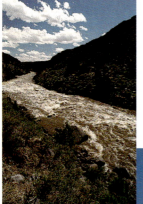

Although many think of New Mexico as a desert state, it is also a land of pine-forested mountains, steep canyons and arroyos, and vast irrigated agricultural lands. The state is configured like a giant wedge, sloping from the Sangre de Cristo Mountains in the north, down past the western ranges to the wide, flat deserts of the southern and eastern parts of the state bordering Texas, Oklahoma, and Mexico. Running north to south, the Rio Grande—"Great River"—roughly bisects the eastern and western halves of the state. Its banks have been settled for centuries—farmed first by ancient Pueblo people, later by the Spanish. ✦

of the north, across the flatlands of New Mexico into Texas. *Photo Stephen Trimble. Right:* Beavertail cactus, near Las Cruces, southern New Mexico. *Photo Eduardo Fuss*

"MOST OF NEW MEXICO, MOST OF THE YEAR, IS AN INDESCRIBABLE harmony in browns and grays, over which the enchanted light of its blue skies casts an eternal spell. Its very rocks are unique…towering across the bare land like the milestones of forgotten giants."

Charles F. Lummis, The Land of Poco Tiempo, *1933*

Landscape, New Mexico by Marsden Hartley, 1920. Hartley described New Mexico as "a country of form, with a new presentation of light as a problem." *Roswell Museum and Art Center*

Rock, Cave, and Canyon

The Ghost of Carlsbad Caverns by Walter Mruk, 1924–25. With its eerie rooms and bizarre rock formations, this vast cavern system feels as if it might well be haunted. *The Harmsen Collection*

Something of a geological marvel, New Mexico boasts a remarkably complete record of geologic history. Every era is represented in its rocks. During the Paleozoic era (570 to 240 million years ago), large parts of the area were submerged beneath ancient seas. The first mountains rose out of these seas, and deposits of marine fossils are found in the high

> *"New Mexico has an austere and planetary look that…challenges the soul."*
>
> Elizabeth Shepley Sergeant

country today. In the southern deserts, marine sediments such as sandstone, limestone, and shale are also remnants of this era. During the Mesozoic era, New Mexico was tropical swampland where dinosaurs and marine life flourished. Finally, during the Cenozoic era (70 million years ago), volcanic activity, along with folding and faulting of the earth's crust, produced New Mexico's great mountain ranges as the seas receded. All this activity left a legacy of unique and fascinating landforms, plus a wealth of rock and mineral deposits.

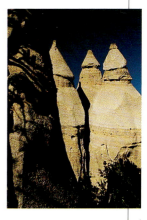

Tent Rocks, in the Jemez Mountains of north-central New Mexico, are the remains of a layer of volcanic tuff, deposited by a massive volcanic explosion about a million years ago, which created the entire mountain range. *Photo Eduardo Fuss. Left:* The lone spire of a yucca plant—"God's candle"—rises dramatically from its bed of white gypsum sand at White Sands National Monument, near Alamogordo. *Photo David Muench*

The first thing most people notice about New Mexico is the quality of the light—a clear, hard-edged light like that found nowhere else. Next is the sky—vast, turquoise blue or piled with thunder clouds, overwhelming. Writer Tony Hillerman says he has seen as many as five thunderstorms at once over the mountains around Santa Fe. The painters of Santa Fe and

VICTOR HIGGINS

A dramatic art installation that pays homage to New Mexico's weather is *The Lightning Field*, created by artist Walter De Maria on a high desert plateau near Quemado. In this lightning-prone area, 400 gleaming steel poles are spaced at regular intervals over about a square mile. During thunderstorms, they act as lightning rods, with spectacular results.

Taos never stopped trying to capture that light and sky; photographers past and present have found it compelling. The farmer is always scanning the sky, hoping for rain. The Native Americans' prayers for rain have always been at the center of their religion. And in the absence of rain, the air can be filled with choking dust, and the desert lies hot and barren. ✦

Opposite: Storm by Victor Higgins, c. 1917–18. *Gerald Peters Gallery* *Above:* Walter De Maria, *The Lightning Field*, 1977. *Dia Center for the Arts Photo John Cliett*

"NEVER IS THE LIGHT MORE PURE AND OVERWEENING than there, arching with a royalty almost cruel over the hollow, uptilted world."

D. H. Lawrence, speaking of Taos, 1931

Cover the heavens
with high-piled clouds
Cover the earth with fog
cover the earth with rains…
cover the earth with lightnings
Let thunder drum over all
    the earth
let thunder be heard
Let thunder drum over all
over all the six directions of
    the earth

Zuni song

"THE SKY WAS AS FULL OF MOTION AND CHANGE AS THE desert beneath it was monotonous and still,—and there was so much sky, more than at sea, more than anywhere else in the world. The plain was there, under one's feet, but what one saw when one looked about was the brilliant blue world of stinging air and moving cloud. Even the mountains were made ant-hills under it. Elsewhere the sky is the roof of the world; but here the earth was the floor of the sky. The landscape one longed for when one was far away, the thing about one, the world one actually lived in, was the sky, the sky."

Willa Cather, Death Comes for the Archbishop, *1927*

Opposite: Church, Buttress, Ranchos de Taos, New Mexico by Paul Strand, 1932. The flat walls and organic forms of New Mexico's adobe structures are lit with dramatic effect under cloud-piled skies. *Aperture Foundation, Inc./ Paul Strand Archive Above:* Rainbow over Acoma pueblo. One of New Mexico's dramatic mesas, Acoma is also home to the fabled "Sky City" pueblo. *Photo Stephen Trimble*

Smokey Bear

The U.S. Forest Service invented Smokey Bear in 1944 to promote awareness of forest fire prevention. "Only YOU can prevent forest fires" became a household phrase. In the aftermath of a forest fire in Capitan, New Mexico, in 1950, firefighters rescued a badly burned bear cub. Nursed back to health, the bear was taken to the National Zoo in Washington, D.C., and became the living symbol of "Smokey."

New Mexico's diverse habitat and climate support a wide variety of animal life, including more than 300 species of birds. Many waterfowl make their homes along the state's irrigation ditches and waterways. Game birds like wild turkey and quail abound, too. And, of course, there's the state bird, the quirky, inquisitive roadrunner. The desert is home to rodents, lizards, snakes, spiders, and scorpions, and that odd relative of the hippopotamus, the javelina. Larger mammals found in the desert and high country include coyotes, deer, and mountain lions.

Practically an emblem of New Mexico, the coyote has been a source of fascination for years. To the Native Americans, Coyote was a pivotal figure in legend—the trickster who created the world and stole fire for the people. In the wild, the coyote is a wily hunter, clever at avoiding capture and, when convenient, at stealing livestock. And its eerie song in the moonlit New Mexican nighttime is something few campers are likely to forget. ✦

"I HAVE TRAILED A COYOTE OFTEN, GOING ACROSS COUNTRY, and found his track such as a man, a very intelligent man accustomed to a hill country,…would make to the same point. Here a detour to avoid a stretch of too little cover, there a pause on the rim of a gully to pick the better way,… and making his point with the greatest economy of effort."

Mary Austin, The Land of Little Rain, 1903

The rich and sophisticated culture of New Mexico's Native Americans has survived nearly intact from ancient times. Everywhere in the state, its powerful influence can be seen and felt. The Native Americans' story begins some 12,000 years ago, when this was still a country of grasslands and forests where nomadic people roamed hunting bison, mammoths, and mastodons. As the Ice Age receded and the climate warmed and dried, a new culture slowly emerged. In the high deserts of northwestern New Mexico, a people collectively known as the Anasazi began to develop an agricultural way of life based on growing corn, beans, and squash. (*Anasazi*, actually a Navajo word, is not used by today's Pueblo people.) This peaceful, settled lifestyle set them apart

Top: Petroglyph from Galisteo Basin, c. 1100 A.D. *Photo David Muench*
Above right: Flint spear point made by the nomadic Clovis people c. 12,000 years ago. *Photo Jerry Jacka. Right:* Moonrise at Pueblo del Arroyo, Chaco Culture National Historic Park. *Photo David Muench*

from many other prehistoric Native Americans and made their great cultural and architectural achievements possible. During a golden era from about A.D. 800 to 1300, the Anasazi built their fabled pueblos—huge cities of rock and adobe centered at Chaco Canyon and other sites. Skilled craftspeople, they created beautiful pottery, jewelry, and weavings. Then, for reasons that remain a mystery, the Anasazi left their magnificent cities in a mass exodus to the south and the east. They built new pueblos in these areas and mixed with other cultures. Today's Pueblo tribes are the descendants of these people. ✛

Hedipa, A Navajo Woman by J. K. Hillers, c. 1880. The nomadic Navajo, later arrivals to New Mexico, were herders and skilled weavers. *University of New Mexico Museum*

"THE MODERN PUEBLO INDIANS...ARE THE DIRECT HEIRS OF A long tradition of human life on this continent....There is no break between their prehistoric past and their present."

Vincent Scully, Pueblo: Mountain, Village, Dance, *1975*

Out of the Earth

The artifacts the ancient ones left behind are evidence of their close ties to things of the earth—the clay soil made into pottery, the rock as "canvas" for painting and raw material for shaping tools and weapons. Corn—the staple food and central to the life of the people—is celebrated in song and in art. The Mogollon, an ancient people from the southwest of New Mexico, created some of the most beautiful early pottery, now called Mimbres after one tribe from that area. The potter's art has continued to flourish throughout Pueblo history.

Ancient Architects

The Anasazi were among the master builders of the ancient world. Many of their dwellings, such as those at what is now Bandelier National Monument, were built along canyon walls and under the edges of cliffs; natural caves in the cliffs were enlarged into rooms. Others were built on the broad, treeless desert or, more rarely, atop mesas. Working in a virtually treeless landscape, the ancient builders hauled timbers over miles of rough terrain without the use of wheels or beasts of burden. They used what they found on the land—rock and clay soil—to fashion roads, buildings, ultimately entire cities that rivaled the work of other ancient peoples such the Aztecs. The structures they created endured into modern times and helped to shape the vocabulary of traditional New Mexican architecture.

Opposite above: Kachina wall painting, Coronodo State Monument. *Photo Eduardo Fuss*
Opposite below: Mimbres black-on-white pottery bowl depicting man catching birds with snare. *Heard Museum. Photo Jerry Jacka*

Left: Masonry wall at Pueblo Bonita, *Chaco Culture National Historic Park. Photo Jerry Jacka*
Above: Elk-Foot of the Taos Tribe by Eanger Irving Couse, c. 1909. *National Museum of American Art/Art Resource*

Map of the Territory of New Mexico, 1851, drawn by expedition artist Richard Kern. *National Archives. Below:* 18th-century "graffiti" carved on Inscription Rock at El Morro National Monument documents the passage of Spanish settlers into New Mexico. Ancient Indian petroglyphs are also carved into the sandstone at this spot. *Photo Stephen Trimble*

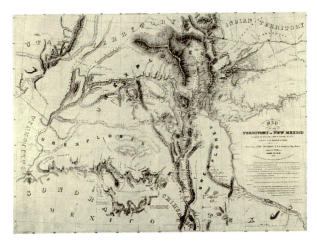

"Here was the General Don Diego de Vargas…

who conquered for our faith and Royal Crown all of New Mexico at his own expense in the year 1692."

Inscription Rock, 1692

With the coming of the Spanish to New Mexico began the gradual interweaving of Spanish arts and crafts, architecture, music, language, religion, and even cooking with that of the Native Americans. In 1540, Francisco Vasquez de Coronado swept into the region, sent by the government of New Spain (Mexico) in search of the fabled Seven Cities of Cibola, rumored to hold a golden treasure like that of the Aztecs. With 300 soldiers, Coronado made the arduous 1,000-mile trek to northern New Mexico, where he found not cities of gold, but pueblos of rock and adobe. He attacked and "conquered" the Zunis, but was forced to return to Mexico empty-handed.

Eventually the Spanish established a successful colonial government in Santa Fe. The new arrivals lost no time in converting the Pueblo people to their own ways, making them wear European-style clothes and worship the Christian God. The Pueblo Revolt of 1680 drove the oppressors from New Mexico for a time, and when the Spanish did return to reconquer the pueblos, they more or less followed a policy of "live and let live." Over the next century, the Spanish established farms and vast ranchos around the New Mexico territory, which as part of Mexico continued under foreign rule until 1821, when Mexico won its independence. ✦

Don Diego de Vargas Zapata y Luján (1643–1704). This elegant gentleman soldier led the reconquest of New Mexico by the Spanish. *Museum of New Mexico*

Vaquero Vocabulary

hacendado	landowner
silla vaquero	Mexican saddle
mochila	saddle cover
espuela	spur
tapaderos	stirrup covers
mesteño	mustang
reata	rope/lariat
armas	chaps

Above: Saddle of Wallace Woodworth, 1855. *Natural History Museum of Los Angeles County, Seaver Center for Western History.* *Below:* Spanish colonial spur, c. 1600, excavated at Pecos Pueblo ruin. *Museum of New Mexico*

The earliest settlers from Mexico became farmers and, later, cattle or sheep ranchers. In the Rio Arriba (upper river) region of the Rio Grande, small homesteads predominated. But along the Rio Abajo, or lower river, the fertile land was owned by a few rich men. Privileged families received large land grants from the Spanish crown; their vast tracts of land were worked by small farmers and—on the cattle ranches—by those romantic Southwestern figures, the *vaqueros,* or cowboys.

The Spanish introduced two novel creatures to New Mexico: the horse, broken for riding, and the cow. The two came together under the vigorous, assertive rule of the *vaquero,* who galloped over the terrain keeping vast herds in line. Natives at first were forbidden to ride horses; later some became skilled *vaqueros* themselves. ✦

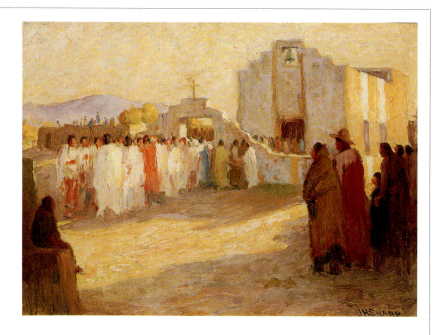

For the Glory of God

The Franciscan friars who accompanied the first wave of Spanish settlers worked zealously to convert the Pueblo people to Christianity. By 1630, they had already established 25 missions in New Mexico. In addition to being converted, the Indians were forced to build churches to the glory of this new God. Many early mission churches are now in ruins; some examples of massive stone and adobe structures, like those at Acoma and Isleta, still stand today.

The Sunset Dance by Joseph Henry Sharp, 1924. Paris-trained painter Sharp captured the timeless pageantry of New Mexico religious life. His enthusiasm for New Mexico brought many other artists of his generation there. *Nedra Matteuci's Fenn Galleries*

View of Santa Fe Plaza in the 1850s by Gerald Cassidy, c. 1930. Santa Fe was the final destination for teams of patient oxen and their plucky drivers. *Museum of New Mexico*

When Mexico gained its independence from Spain in 1821, the gates to New Mexico were opened to Americans from the East. Over the Santa Fe Trail they came, across 800 grueling and dangerous miles from Missouri all the way to the remote little Spanish-Indian town of Santa Fe. A fearless trader named William Becknell led the way in

1822, and scores of eager traders followed his example, along with the adventurers and mountain men who supplied animal hides for trade. The trip from Missouri took two or three long months; the travelers faced starvation, raging thirst, and Indian attacks—but still they came. In places, the ruts made by their wheels can still be seen, carved deep into the New Mexican soil. Settlers followed the traders, and the invasion of New Mexico by the Anglos had begun.

After the Mexican War of 1846–47, New Mexico became a U.S. Territory. Under the 1848 Treaty of Guadalupe Hidalgo, New Mexico was formally ceded to the United States. But the territory remained an outpost, beleaguered by skirmishes with the Navajo and Apache, and by lawlessness among the Anglos. After a long struggle, New Mexico finally joined the Union as a state in 1912. ⚜

The Ox-Driving Song

On the fourteenth day of October-o
I hitched my team in order-o
To drive to the hills of Saludio.
To me rol to me rol to me ride-o.

When I got there the hills were steep,
T'would make a tender-hearted person weep,
To hear me cuss and pop my whip,
To see my oxen pull and slip.

When I get home I'll have revenge,
I'll land my family among my friends.
I'll bid adieu to the whip and line,
And drive no more in the wintertime.

A driving song of the "bull whackers" whose teams hauled freight along the Santa Fe Trail and other routes to the growing settlements of the West

Portrait of Kit Carson, Indian fighter, trailblazer, and scout. Colonel Carson was one of the Southwest's legendary figures. *Kit Carson Historic Museums*

"I'll sing you the song of Billy the Kid...

I'll sing of the desperate deed that he did;
Way out in New Mexico long, long ago,
When a man's only chance was his old forty-four."

Song quoted in New Mexico *(WPA Guide)*

New Mexico's most notorious outlaw was Billy the Kid. His short but violent career included dramatic jailbreaks and cold-blooded murder. He met his own death in 1881 at age 21, at the hands of Sheriff Pat Garrett. On the other side of the law was the legendary Elfego Baca, sheriff of Socorro County. Baca once held off a con-

Above: Billy the Kid (Henry Antrim, a.k.a. Henry McCarty, a.k.a. William Bonney). Illustration by Bob Boze Bell, 1992, from *The Illustrated Life and Times of Billy the Kid. Courtesy of the artist. Right:* Lawman Elfego Baca proudly displays the gun he stole from the legendary Pancho Villa. *Museum of New Mexico*

tingent of 80 cowboys bent on releasing a prisoner; holed up inside a plaster hut for 36 hours, he emerged unharmed when a deputy arrived. His prowess was celebrated in the 1958 Walt Disney movie *The Nine Lives of Elfego Baca*. ✧

The Old Santa Fe Trail by William Herbert Dunton, c. 1920–22. The Burlington Northern Santa Fe Railway Company Art Collection

"PUBLIC GAMBLING WAS BOTH THE LEADING INDUSTRY AND THE leading sport in Santa Fe…Liquor was cheap, women were bought and sold like horses, and almost everyone carried arms."

A visitor during the 1840s, in Richard Erdoes, Saloons of the Old West, *1979*

The Anglo-Americans came to New Mexico for every kind of reason—quick profit, adventure, the feel of the open country, a new start in life, and the lure of a history and culture different from the one they had known. Not just adventurers but plenty of respectable folk came to try their hands at farming, mining, ranching, and trades in the growing towns. Many of them strove to bring to their new lives the familiar order and "standards" of the lives they had left behind. Others fell under the spell of the new territory and, drawn to the ways of those who had come before, found themselves forever changed by the encounter. ✢

Above: Zuni silver pin with mother of pearl, turquoise, and jet, c. 1950. *Morning Star Gallery. Photo Addison Doty. Below:* Boss Saloon and Concert Hall, Albuquerque, New Mexico, 1897. At the turn of the century, saloons were still a gathering place for New Mexicans. *University of New Mexico Photo Eddie Ross Cobb and William Henry Cobb Opposite above: Santa Fe in the 1880s by Frances X. Grosshenney, c. 1880. Museum of New Mexico Opposite below: The Cliff Mine in Senorito, photograph by Henry Schmidt, c. 1900. University of New Mexico*

Treasure from the Earth

Mining was important in New Mexico's early development and still features in its economy. In fact, New Mexico had its own gold rush, 20 years before California's; the Sierra del Oro, now called the Ortiz Mine, yielded the first strike in 1833. But the state's most treasured mineral is turquoise. First mined by Pueblo Indians centuries ago, the sky-blue stone is prized for its color and richly veined patterns. Along the famed Turquoise Trail, between Albuquerque and Santa Fe, are many mining sites—some played out and some still active. Gold, silver, copper, lead, and zinc have also come out of these hills.

Taos Farmers by Catherine Carter Critcher, c. 1929. *The San Antonio Art League Opposite: Furrowed Fields* by Paul Burlin, 1915. *University of Nebraska, Sheldon Memorial Art Gallery, Howard S. Wilson Memorial Collection*

Water—or its absence—determines where and how people live on the land in New Mexico. In the high country, there may be 30 inches of rainfall a year; along the Rio Grande, maybe 10 inches—and in the true desert less still. When it does rain, it's often in sudden storms that flood and overwhelm young plants. In such a land, farming is a challenge to human ingenuity and perseverance. But the Native Americans and Spanish who first settled here have been well versed in the art of dry-farming for centuries. The Pueblo Indians learned to coax from the land basic crops—corn, beans, squash, and chiles—by inventing unique irrigation systems of small dams and canals or ditches, with mud walls. When rain created floodwaters, these networks directed water from overflowing streams to the crops. The Spanish farmers renamed these irrigation canals *acequias*. A main, or "mother," ditch, the *acequia madre*, was dug and maintained by the community. This fed into smaller ditches that served individual fields. ✦

"Now what is a man but his earth?...

It rises in walls to shelter him in life. it sinks to receive him at death. By eating its corn he builds his flesh into walls of this selfsame earth. He has its granitic hardness or its soft resiliency. He is different as each field even is different. Thus do I know my own earth; I can know no other. I am greedy for my land, and that is right. Does not a child cry for its mother's breasts?"

Frank Waters, People of the Valley, *1941*

Over your field
  of growing corn,
All day shall hang
  the thundercloud.
Over your field
  of growing beans
All day shall come
  the rousing rain!

Traditional Pueblo song

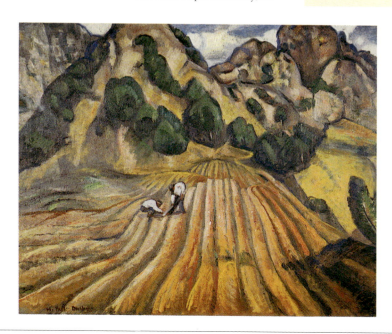

The Spanish introduced to New Mexico sheep and cattle—breeds that could endure hot, dry conditions. Merino sheep, brought to New Mexico by colonists in 1598, were the dominant force in its agricultural economy until the cattle industry took hold in the 19th century. Native Americans, especially the Navajos, tended herds of sheep that supplied them with the raw material for their celebrated blankets and other weavings. On Spanish ranchos, the owners of huge tracts of land often employed herders on a *partidario* basis, whereby the "sharecropper" in effect rented the sheep and gave over a percentage (usually a large one) of lambs and wool to the owner.

Cattle ranching was (and is) big business in New Mexico. In the old days of the cattle drive, herds of beef cattle raised on the Llano Estacado ("staked plains") and other areas found their way to shipping points along the old "hoof highways." The "Beefsteak Trail," used from 1885 into the 1950s, headed across New Mexico for the railhead at Magdalena. Both the Chisum Trail to Arizona and the famous Goodnight–Loving Trail to Colorado passed through Roswell, New Mexico; during the heyday of the cattle drive, the town was a major cattle center in the Southwest. ✤

"A PERSON WHO HAS NEVER SLEPT OR EATEN AROUND A CHUCK wagon with a large cow outfit, who has never gone on a circle drive, ridden a well-trained 'cuttin' horse' in a roundup, day herded, roped or flanked calves around a branding fire, or stood guard around a sleeping or milling herd…has missed some of the most vivid experiences of the Old West."

V. H. Whitlock ("Ol'Waddy), Cowboy Life on the Llano Estacado, 1970

An Afternoon of the Sheep Herder by Ernest L. Blumenschein, 1939. The artist was spellbound by the drama of the landscape and the character of its inhabitants. *National Cowboy Hall of Fame and Western Heritage Center*

Above: New Mexico red chile. *Photo Eduardo Fuss. Below: The Chile Blanket,* woven by the Pendleton Woolen Mills. *Opposite: Making Chile Ristras by Diana Bryer, 1989. Courtesy of the artist*

Green or ripened red, fiery or mild, the chile pepper is the basis of great New Mexican cooking as well as an important crop. Chiles are the magic ingredient that lend bite and savor to New Mexico's unforgettable salsas and its most notable dishes—from posole to carne adovada. The chile was cultivated by Pueblo peoples for centuries and enthusiastically adopted by the Spanish and Anglo arrivals. It's more popular today than ever; and many claim that New Mexico's flavorful chiles are in a class by themselves. In pepper-growing country, roadside stands sell fresh varieties, and harvest time in late summer and autumn infuses the air with the rich, smoky aroma of roasting peppers. All over New Mexico, chiles are strung to dry in ristras, those garlands that hang so picturesquely from weathered timbers or adobe walls. ✤

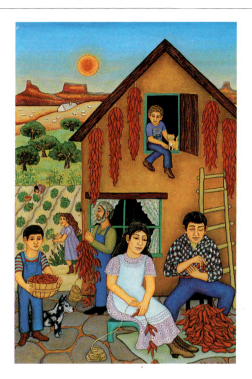

Green Chile Chutney

2 pounds fresh New Mexico green
    chiles, roasted, peeled, and diced
    (or roasted Anaheim chiles,
    with 2 or 3 roasted jalapeños)
2 cups sugar
1 tablespoon roasted ground New
    Mexico oregano
⅔ cup cider vinegar
1 teaspoon salt

Mix the ingredients together and cook
for 10 to 15 minutes over medium heat
in an enamel or stainless steel pan.
Allow to cool, and serve cold. For a
hotter chutney, add 6 diced roasted
jalapeños (or increase the number
accordingly if using Anaheims and
jalapeños). Yield: 4 cups.

Mark Miller, The Great Chile Book

THE FLAVOR OF NEW MEXICO'S CHILES IS
"…unlike that of any other chile in
North America: sweet and earthy, with
a clarity that seems to reflect the skies
and landscapes of New Mexico."

*Mark Miller, Southwestern cuisine guru and
proprietor of Santa Fe's renowned Coyote Cafe,
in* The Great Chile Book, *1991*

Talking Chiles

ancho (dried *poblano*)	Numex Big Jim
chimayó	New Mexico No. 6
jalapeño	*poblano*
New Mexico green	*sandia*
New Mexico red	Santa Fe grande
	serrano

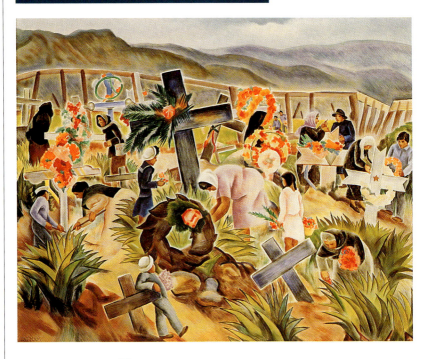

Decoration Day by Barbara Latham, c. 1935. Latham, a painter and printmaker, moved to Taos in the 1930s. Much of her work shows her fascination with Pueblo ceremonies and the spiritual life of Hispanic New Mexico. *Harwood Museum*

Religion is woven closely into the fabric of New Mexican life. The Native American beliefs, so intimately linked with the rhythms of nature, have been an integral part of Pueblo culture since ancient times. Then and now, faith is expressed in dance, in rituals within the ceremonial kiva, and in many aspects of Native arts. Roman Catholicism, brought from Mexico by the Spanish, takes on a special character here because of the Hispanic people's deep ties to the land. This faith has always been expressed in church ritual and celebrations such as saint's day fiestas, as well as in a wealth of religious art and architecture. Over the centuries, the Catholic faith has blended with that of the Pueblo people to create a rich blend of religions that is uniquely New Mexican. In addition, a general feeling of tolerance and openness has from time to time attracted special or unusual religious sects to New Mexico's mountains and canyons. ✤

Untitled by Emil Bisttram, 1933. The stylized ceremonial masks and body paint displayed by the Zuni dancers, Koshares, are depicted here; these "clowns" are key figures in religious ceremonies. *Museum of Fine Arts, Museum of New Mexico*

"AND ALL THE WHILE THE KOSHARES pantomined the insistent prayer… Two of them were divided vertically with paint….The other nine were just alike….Their ashy grey bodies were splotched with white and black spots, their faces weirdly streaked with zigzag lines….So beautiful of movement as they weaved continually through the lines of unheeding dancers like alert, spotted leopards…. Their loose flexible arms with poetic gestures drew up the deep power from the blackness of the earth with which they were painted…."

Frank Waters, Masked Gods: Navaho and Pueblo Ceremonialism, *1950*

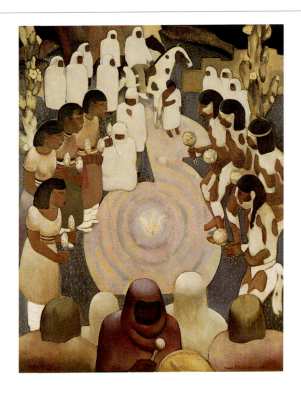

"THIS IS THE DANCE OF THE SPROUTING CORN, AND EVERYBODY HOLDS A LITTLE, BEATING branch of green pine. Thud-thud-thud-thud-thud! goes the drum, heavily the men hop and hop and hop, sway, sway, sway, sway go the little branches of green pine. It tosses like a little forest, and the deep sound of men's singing is like the booming and tearing of a wind deep inside a forest. They are dancing the Spring Corn Dance.... And the mystery of germination...life springing within the seed, is accomplished."

D. H. Lawrence, The Dance of the Sprouting Corn, *1924*

Sacred Rituals and Images

The sacred dances of the Pueblos are prayers and supplications, celebrations and expressions of gratitude and awe toward the powers of nature. Intricate and precise, they have followed the same forms for centuries. The spring Corn Dance at Taos Pueblo is performed in May.

While the term *santos* has been applied to all sacred art created by the Spanish in New Mexico, the classic carved icons of the Spanish Colonial period are properly called *bultos*. These beautiful images, usually depicting saints, were carved from pine or cottonwood, coated with gesso, and painted with tempera. Fetishes carved in the images of animals—turtles, owls, bears, rabbits, and other wildlife—express the deep connection that Native American people feel with their fellow creatures. These charming carvings of marble, turquoise, horn, or other materials are often created simply as art. But if blessed by a shaman, they become "true" fetishes, with the power to protect, to cure, or perhaps to bring good fortune in an endeavor such as hunting.

Opposite: Corn Dance, Taos Pueblo by Norman Chamberlain, 1934. *National Museum of American Art/Art Resource Left:* Bear fetish in black sandstone by Lance Yazzie, Navajo. *Photo*

Jerry Jacka. Above: San Jose, santos figure by Marie Romero Cash, 1985. Among New Mexico's earliest art forms, these carvings are prized by collectors. *Photo Eduardo Fuss*

Travel along the Santa Fe and other trails into and out of New Mexico improved all through the mid-1800s with the coming of better wagons, stronger mules, and eventually the stagecoach and Pony Express services. Meanwhile, rail surveys determined that routes through New Mexico were feasible, and the first trains entered the state in the fall of 1879. The Santa Fe Railroad eventually reached Albuquerque and beyond, linking up with the Southern Pacific, while the Denver and Rio Grande line snaked down from Colorado. The coming of the railroads transformed New Mexican life, bringing vastly more settlers and stimulating industry. New towns were built, great ranches established, mines opened, and land values boomed.

The railroads made it possible for the first time to build with non-native materials, and in the late 19th century, buildings in the Victorian and other period styles began to appear in New Mexico. The state's unique architectural heritage, formed by Pueblo and Spanish influences, was threatened for a time; even Santa Fe's venerable Palace of

the Governors underwent a Victorian facelift. But members of the arts community and other citizens launched a successful movement to preserve and promote the native adobe, Spanish Colonial, and Territorial styles so visually and climatically suited to the setting. Later structures like the New Mexico State Art Museum reflect this trend. Today, in a world of mass-produced, lookalike public buildings, New Mexico's distinctive built environment is central to the state's appeal. ✦

In the 1944 film *The Harvey Girls*, Judy Garland portrayed a waitress in one of the West's celebrated Harvey Houses. *Photofest/Jagarts Opposite above:* Drawing by P. C. Napolitano in *Operations Santa Fe Opposite below:* U.S. postage stamp depicting the Palace of the Governors in its restored form.

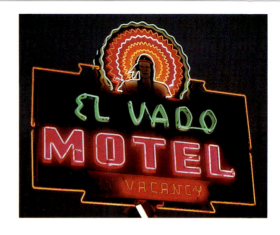

Right and below: Neon splendor along Route 66 and a New Mexico state decal. *Decal courtesy Michael Wallis, photo Terrence Moore. Opposite above:* Museum of Fine Arts, Santa Fe. Designed in 1917 by architects Rapp and Rapp, it took inspiration from missions around the state. *Photo Jack Parsons. Opposite below:* Sculpture of J. Robert Oppenheimer by the Schwartz Brothers, New York, 1981. *Bradbury Science Museum, Los Alamos Photo Jack Parsons*

Kicks on Route 66

The last road signs for Route 66 were taken down in 1985, but in its heyday the legendary highway stretched from Chicago across the nation, passing through Albuquerque and Gallup before running on into Arizona. Millions of motorists got their first, wide-open glimpse of the Southwest driving along this grand old road. Between long stretches across empty desert and open country, it passed outposts of mom-and-pop stores and gas stations, cafes, and motor courts, and slowed the motorist down through small countless small towns. John Steinbeck's Joad family, as well as real-life Dust Bowl migrants, also followed Route 66 on their way to California, or anyplace they could find work. Steinbeck called Route 66 the "mother road"; to others it is "America's Main Street." Though in ruins, it still exists in the memories of many who traveled it in the "good old days" before superhighways.

> "WE WERE VERY ISOLATED. THERE was only a ribbon of 66 going through these parts. That was our touch with the world."
>
> *Ron Chavez, club owner, Santa Rosa*
> *in* Route 66: The Mother Road

Secrets in the Desert

In 1941, in the pine-forested mesa country of Pajarito Plateau, scientists from all over the country gathered in secret to work on what we now know as the Manhattan Project—the development of the world's first atomic bomb. J. Robert Oppenheimer, a U.C. Berkeley physics professor, remembered the site from a pack trip he had taken 20 years earlier, and recommended it as a sufficiently out-of-the-way site for their secret work. In July of 1945, the first atomic bomb was detonated at Trinity Site, 60 miles south of Alamagordo.

Front door, Camino del Monte Sol, Santa Fe. *Photo Jack Parsons. Below: Angel Trestero,* hand-made painted wood cabinet by Jim Wagner. *The Parks Gallery*

The interiors of New Mexican homes are often as distinctive as their adobe walls. Architectural details such as ceilings and fireplaces, as well as furnishings, have a style all their own. In the haciendas of Spanish Colonial times, interior details and furniture were made by hand from simple, traditional designs. Over the years, these designs were copied, adapted, and embellished by later craftsmen. Great interest in interior design was part of the renaissance in New Mexican arts and crafts inspired by the Santa Fe and Taos artists' colony in the 1920s. Noted craftspeople such as William Penhallow Henderson created exquisite handmade pieces—couches, chests, beds, chairs, tables, and cupboards—modeled on Spanish Colonial designs. Home design that combines classic and embellished Spanish designs with Native American influences has been dubbed the "Santa Fe Style." This unique New Mexican "look" continues to be reworked and reinvented—and remains as popular as ever. ❖

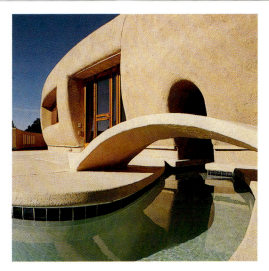

"INSIDE THE HOUSE THERE IS THE SAME swept and almost barren look. A large bed adorns the living room, and a few upright chairs stand upon the mud floor. In 1917 there was always a hand-made Santo or two up on the walls, and in most of the houses there were old carved boxes that had been wedding chests and then became granaries...."

Mabel Dodge Luhan, An Escape to Reality, *1937*

Many of the classic New Mexican fiber arts such as weaving and stitchery are rooted in the arts and crafts of the Spanish Colonial period. The techniques were brought up from Mexico (many had their origins in Spain). Native American influences contributed new materials and techniques in some cases, as with weaving. And the availability of certain raw materials—metals, for example—often determined the direction taken by crafts like ironwork and tinsmithing. As Anglo influence increased through the nineteenth century, many of the old techniques were all but lost. Fortunately, many were revived through the efforts of the Spanish Colonial Arts Society in the 1920s, and later, the New Deal's Federal Arts Project. Today, gifted craftspeople are creating new work based on traditional techniques and designs. ✢

Above: A pine chair crafted in 1917 by Jesse Nussbaum is among the earliest examples of Spanish Colonial Revival furniture in New Mexico. *Museum of New Mexico*

Photo Mary Peck. Left: Tin mirror with wallpaper insert by Emilio and Senaida Romero, 1988. *Museum of International Folk Art. Photo Michel Monteaux*

"*The glamorous tradi-
tion of the Hacienda
lives on in the highly
skilled crafts of the
Spanish-American.*

…His creations will lend
your home its most dis-
tinctive touch."

*1930s ad for the Southwestern Master
Craftsmen company in Santa Fe*

"THE CRAFT REVIVAL OFFERED THE POSSIBILITY
of preserving the local [Hispanic] community in
which the spiritual values and creative powers of
the people could thrive."

William Wroth, in Revivals! Diverse Traditions, 1920–1945, *1994*

Sopa de Frijoles
(Black Bean Soup)

1 ½ cups dried black beans
1 tbs sunflower oil
4 oz back bacon, chopped
1 large onion, chopped
1 garlic clove, crushed
2 or 3 green jalapeño chiles,
   seeded and chopped
2 tomatoes, peeled and chopped
2 ½ cups vegetable stock
Fresh cilantro, sprigs and leaves
Salt and pepper

Cover beans with cold water, soak overnight. Drain, cover with water in large pan, bring to boil, boil rapidly for 15 minutes. Drain and reserve. Heat oil in casserole and sauté bacon, onion, garlic, and chiles for 5 minutes; stir occasionally. Add beans, tomatoes, and stock. Bring to boil, reduce heat, add cilantro sprigs and seasoning to taste. Gently simmer 1 hour or until beans are tender. Remove sprigs, check seasoning, garnish with chopped cilantro. Serves 4.

Adapted from Gina Steer,
The Great Chile Pepper Cookbook

A selection of New Mexico's distinctive beans.
Photo FoodPix

Among American's regional cuisines, the food of the Southwest—of New Mexico in particular—has great appeal these days. Restaurant chefs and home cooks are having a love affair with this distinctive style of cooking, reinterpreting it in countless fresh ways as well as enjoying its traditional dishes. The basic ingredients are simple: corn, beans, chiles, squash, and piñon nuts, as well as beef—all products of the New Mexican land. The dishes prepared with these staples come largely from Mexican-Spanish cookery. They were brought to New Mexico during the era of settlement and adapted to the local crops. The Spanish also borrowed from Native American cooking. Today, traditional foods like posole, salsa, and sopapillas are joined by exciting new creations in a cuisine that's ever changing and ever delicious. ✤

Baking bread, Laguna Pueblo, c. 1930s. The traditional clay *horno*, the outdoor oven of the pueblos, was introduced by the Spanish in the 17th century. *Underwood Photo Archives, Inc.*

"You let the fire die down and rake out

the hot ashes. In goes one of your precious chickens and the bread. The board that serves as a door is quickly closed, and the large stone put against it. Then you sit down and wait."

Dorothy Brett, Lawrence and Brett, 1933

"Mud is the flesh of the earth, and stones are the bones."

Anita Rodriguez, *quoted in* The Desert Is No Lady, *1987*

Conjure an image of New Mexico, and you instantly picture buildings made of adobe. This mixture of sand, clay, and water has been in use since ancient times. In a land where trees are scarce or must be hauled from a long way off, adobe was the material of choice. It was easy to work with and pro-

duced walls with excellent insulating properties. The Native Americans used a technique called "puddled adobe," patting and shaping the mixture into long bands, one on top of another. When the Spanish came, they introduced the practice of adobe brick-making. After the advent of wheat as a crop, brickmakers added straw to the bricks, for greater strength.

Adobe continues to evolve, as a material and a style. Its warm tones and organic form, harmonizing so well with the New Mexican land-scape, have made it a favorite with contemporary architects—as well as with generations of artists who portray it in their paintings. ✧

Adobe detail, Mission Church, Ranchos de Taos. *Photo Stephen Trimble. Opposite: The Plasterer* by Ernest L. Blumenschein, 1921. The artist modeled this somber and sympathetic figure on Taos handyman Epiminso Tenorio. *Eiteljorg Museum of Western Art*

"WHEN IT WAS TIME TO COVER THE WALLS WITH plaster—first rough, then smooth—the Pueblo people sent word that they wanted to do it. The men mixed the mud and carried it inside to the women. Some kneaded it and handed it to those who, with skilled hands, covered the adobe bricks. There was much talk and laughter and always a beautiful rainbow motion of the hand, so that I look now at the walls and see those plastering days as a rainbow."

Peggy Pond Church, The House at Otowi Bridge, *1959*

An Adobe House

A house born of the brown earth
and dying back to earth again,
Without any desire to be more
    than earth
and without any particular pain,
Beside an acequia bringing water
to corn not yet tall.

Witter Bynner, Indian Earth, *1929*

The pottery, weaving, and jewelry produced by Native American craftspeople is often of such fine workmanship and design that it steps from craft into the realm of fine art. Traditionally, artists gather materials from the land—vegetable dyes for rugs made of wool from their own sheep, or clay for pottery—and such acts are an integral part of creating the object.

Today many artists combine these old traditions with modern techniques and ideas to create works that honor both. ✢

Silver bolo clasp inlaid with turquoise, coral, jet, and gold-lip mother-of-pearl, by Zuni artists Alex and Marylita Boone.

Navajo "chief's blanket," c. 1890–1910. The art of weaving finds its most widespread expression among the Navajo, who probably learned from the Pueblo people. Older blankets were dyed with the subtle colors of plant material. In the 1880s, brightly colored, predyed yarn from the East was introduced, and "eye-dazzler" blankets became standard. *Arizona State Museum. All photos, these pages, Jerry Jacka*

Left: Pottery jar by Maria Martinez and Popovi Da, San Ildefonso Pueblo. In the 1920s, the esteemed potter Maria Martinez and her family created lustrous black pottery with designs inscribed into its surface, now prized the world over. *Private collection*

Below: Storyteller figure by Helen Cordero, Cochiti Pueblo. In the 1800s, with the coming of the railroad, Cochiti potters created clay figurines that gently mocked the cowboys, businessmen, and others "invading" their land. Cordero introduced her "storytellers" in the 1960s. *The Heard Museum*

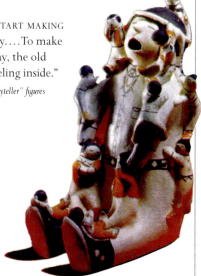

"I DON'T JUST GET UP IN THE MORNING AND START MAKING potteries. First, I go and talk to Grandma Clay....To make good potteries, you have to do it the right way, the old way, and you have to have a special happy feeling inside."

Helen Cordero, creator of "storyteller" figures

They wear squash-flowers cut in silver
And carve the sun on canyon walls;
Their words are born of storm and calyx,
Eagles, and waterfalls.

They weave the thunder in the basket,
And paint the lightning in the bowl;
Taking the village to the rainbow,
The rainbow to the soul.

Haniel Long

New Art from Old Traditions

Although Native American painting had early origins in rock art, it was not a common medium of expression among New Mexican Indians until the early 20th century. In the 1920s, young artists from San Ildefonso, Tesuque, Zia, and other pueblos began to attend art school at the Museum of New Mexico, at Santa Fe. For many years, U.S. federal policy restricted expressions of Indian culture, but this was relaxed in the 1930s, partly because of the efforts of Mary Austin and others in the Santa Fe and Taos art colonies. A flowering of Indian painting followed; artists such as Awa Tsireh, Crescencio Martinez, Pop Chalee, and Tonita Peña (Quah Ah) eventually showed their work all over the country. Sculpture as fine art is a more recent phenomenon among Southwestern native peoples.

Left: Maiden, **bronze by Dan Namingha, 1995. This sculptor and painter draws on images from his Hopi–Tewa heritage to create art that is distinctly contemporary in feeling and treatment.** *Niman Fine Art, Santa Fe. Above: Ozone Madonna* **by Bob Haozous, 1989.** *The Heard Museum. Opposite above: Blue Night at Mount Taylor* **by Emmi Whitehorse, 1986.** *AICA Gallery, San Francisco. Opposite below: Navajo Woman* **by R. C. Gorman, 1973.** *The Heard Museum, Phoenix*

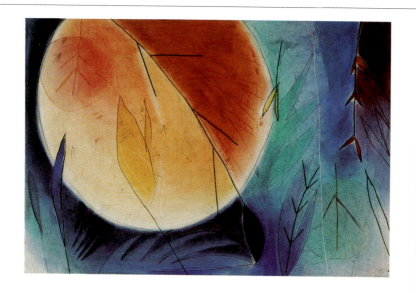

Today's artists—Dan Namingha, Linda Lomahaftewa, Emmi Whitehorse, R. C. Gorman, Bob Haozous, and others—have achieved major standing in the contemporary arts world.

"IN THE DREAMY WORKS OF [EMMI] WHITEHORSE, we may detect a living life-line to her Navajo inheritance....This well-schooled abstractionist, however, can't help but translate her aboriginal unconscious into art that is fully contemporary and globally intelligible."

Jan E. Adlmann, Contemporary Art in New Mexico, *1996*

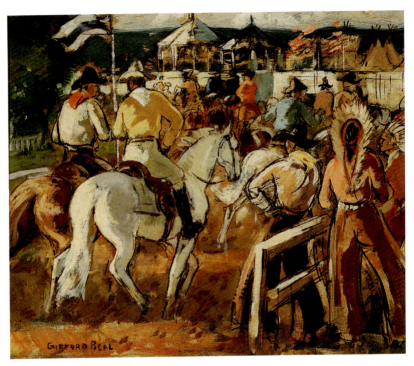

Rodeo by Gifford Beal, 1943. Once informal gatherings of working cowhands, the rodeo has evolved into a highly competitive sport.
*The Anschutz Collection
Photo W. O'Connor*

That most colorful of celebrations—the fiesta—came to New Mexico by way of Mexico. Some fiestas are saint's days that honor the Roman Catholic patron saints of the villages; others are civic in origin. One of the most venerable is the Fiesta de Santa Fe, originally held in memory of Don Diego de Vargas, who claimed New

The fiesta dress, a confection of ruffles and rickrack loosely based on 19th-century Mexican clothing, was popularized in the 1920s and has enjoyed repeated fashion renaissances, especially in the 1950s. *Photo Eduardo Fuss. Below: Vaquero by Luis Jimenez, Jr., modeled 1980, cast 1990. National Museum of American Art/Art Resource*

Mexico for the Spanish in 1692. A tradition since 1712, it's the oldest community celebration in the country. Spanish dancers and mariachis, candlelight processions and decorations in the Plaza mark this festival in September. A high point is the burning of Zozobra, a 40-foot figure constructed of chicken wire and papier-mâché. He is a symbol of gloom and bad luck; as the fire consumes him, it also symbolically devours bad fortune and gives fiesta-goers a fresh start. ✦

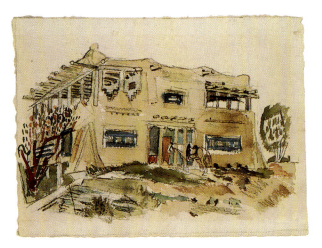

The Marin House, John's Horse Jack, Mabel Luhan Estate by John Marin, 1929. Kennedy Galleries Inc., New York. Below: *Mabel Dodge Looking at the Sanchez Kid* by Jim Wagner, 1981. From *Jim Wagner, Taos, An American Artist.* Rancho Milagro Productions

The art colonies that sprang up in Santa Fe and Taos at the turn of the century embraced all forms, including literature, drama, music, and dance. Many writers and other creative people who flocked to the area were lured by the influential Mabel Dodge Luhan, a wealthy New Yorker with a keen appreciation for art and a penchant for "collecting" artists. Writers were also attracted to New Mexico by the need to break free from the materialism and hurly-burly of life in the cities; they sought a milieu conducive to self-expression and reflection. Besides, for many "starving artists," New Mexico was an inexpensive

place to live. Some took the land and culture of New Mexico as their themes; others were content to let the land nurture them while they worked. Among the writers who lived or spent time in New Mexico were D. H. Lawrence, Oliver LaFarge, Mary Austin, Willa Cather, and Robinson Jeffers.

New Mexico's literary tradition is still going strong; contemporary authors include Tony Hillerman, Rudolfo Anaya, John Nichols, Native American poets Leslie Silko and Simon Ortiz, and many others. ✤

"I THINK NEW MEXICO WAS THE greatest experience from the outside world that I have ever had. It certainly changed me for ever. Curious as it may sound, it was New Mexico that liberated me from the present era of civilization, the great era of material and mechanical development....The moment I saw the brilliant, proud morning shine high up over the deserts of Santa Fe, something stood still in my soul…"

D. H. Lawrence, "New Mexico," 1931

Above left: Cover of Willa Cather's *Death Comes for the Archbishop,* from a drawing by Harold Von Schmidt. *Above:* New Mexico native Frank Waters authored *The Book of the Hopi* and many other works. *Photo Cradoc Bagshaw Left:* Portrait of D. H. Lawrence, c. 1922–23. The British writer and his wife, Frieda, lived in New Mexico on and off from 1922 to 1926. Lawrence reveled in his surroundings, where he produced short fiction, poetry, and essays. *Center for Southwest Research, University of New Mexico*

Right: Photograph from the Santa Fe Players 1919 production, *The Man Who Married a Dumb Wife,* directed by Mary Austin. *Museum of New Mexico. Below:* Mary Austin, c. 1914, referred to behind her back as "God's mother-in-law," reigned supreme over the Santa Fe literary scene during the 1920s. *Museum of New Mexico*

Drama in the Desert

Theater played a part in the flowering of the New Mexican arts colonies. In the early 20th century, Santa Fe had two theaters. A local dramatic group called the Santa Fe Players produced plays written by resident artists such as poet Witter Bynner, as well as standard repertoire. Play readings were also popular in the 1930s; playwright Lynn Riggs often read for these from his own works, such as *Rancour* and *Knives from Syria.*

Ballet and modern dance flourished along with the other lively arts in the Santa Fe and Taos colonies. Writer and community leader Mary Austin was a modern dance enthusiast; she entertained the legendary Martha Graham at her Santa Fe home in 1932 and helped foster local interest in dance. Performers who came to Santa Fe included Graham company dancer Irene Emory and Anna Duncan, a protégé of Isadora Duncan.

Made for the Movies

Much of New Mexico's landscape has become familiar to people who have never set foot in the state, but have seen it time and again on the silver screen. The mesas and cañons of the Gallup area, in particular, have made perfect backdrops for Western movies from the 1930s into the present. And the small farming town of Truchas, at the foot of Truchas Peaks, was the setting for Robert Redford's 1980s film, *The Milagro Beanfield War,* based on the novel by New Mexican John Nichols.

Built by the great D. W. Griffith's brother, R. E., in 1937, the El Rancho Hotel housed stars such as Lionel Barrymore, Burt Lancaster, Betty Grable, and others who came to make movies in New Mexico. Albuquerque's Kimo Theater has been dubbed "Pueblo Deco" because of its flamboyant mix of Pueblo Revival and Art Deco styles. First built as one of the great "moving picture palaces" of the 1920s, it has been restored and now enjoys a new life as a performing arts center.

Lobby doorhandles, Kimo Theater, Albuquerque. *Photo Eduardo Fuss Below:* Scene from the film *The Milagro Beanfield War,* the story of a big landowner's clash with a local Hispanic community. *Photo Elliott Marks/Photofest*

Right: Soprano Sheri Greenawald sings the role of L'Aurora in *L'Egisto* by Pier Francesco Cavalli, at the Santa Fe Opera, 1976. Santa Fe has been called "the Salzburg of the U.S." because its summer opera festival is an international destination. *Photo Ken Howard, Santa Fe Opera. Below:* Taos and Cochiti pueblos are noted for their traditional drums. *Courtesy Taos Drums. Photo Pat Pollard*

Like all of New Mexico's arts, its music reflects a trio of cultures—Native American, Spanish, and Anglo. The musical traditions of the Pueblos are rooted in religion and associated with religious dances. A vibrant strain of Spanish and Mexican folk songs, as well as ecclesiastical music, is everywhere evident. Cowboy and trail songs, which spring from this tradition as well as the Anglo experience, are also central to New Mexican music. In recent history, folk music has evolved into

Country & Western, and on into rock and roll—which has important roots in the area. On the other side of the musical tracks, the Santa Fe Opera and the Santa Fe Chamber Orchestra have made major contributions to the world of classical music.

Spanish Strains

Music was integral to the lives of the Spanish who came to New Mexico. With the missions came sacred music, as well as the deep, mellow tones of the church bells brought up from Mexico. But it was popular music that lent sparkle to the daily life of the villages and haciendas. In most families there was someone who could play the violin, the flute, or the guitar (*vihuela*), and enthusiastic singers abounded. Two types of song—the *canciones* (lyrical ballads) and the *alabadas* (sacred songs)—prevailed. Singing and dancing were a lively part of fiestas held year round.

The Guitarist by Joseph A. Fleck, c. 1932–38. Austrianborn, Fleck came to Taos in 1924 after seeing a show of Taos Society artists in Kansas City. He painted through the 1950s from his studio near the Ranchos de Taos church, seen as a vignette in this painting of a local guitarist. Musicians were among his favorite subjects; the church was another. *Museum of Fine Arts, Museum of New Mexico*

A Composer in Santa Fe

Composer Ernest Bloch spent considerable time among the artists of the Santa Fe colony; in 1924 he composed seven works there, including portions of his symphony *America*. He said, "The people of Santa Fe had more real music than we have in our artificial cities.... Then the Indians! What an extraordinary impression they made upon me with their beautiful music."

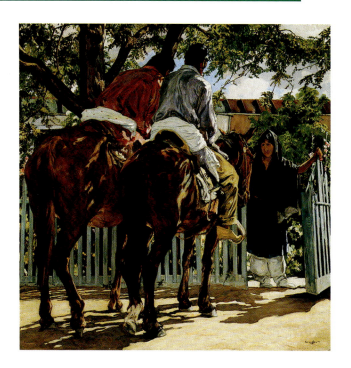

The seeds of New Mexico's fabled arts colonies were sown by serendipity one day in 1898. A young painter named Ernest L. Blumenschein was bumping along a mountain road near Taos in a wagon with fellow painter Bert Phillips. When a wheel broke, Blumenschein sought help in Taos, 20 miles away. Limping into town, he was immediately captivated by what he saw. The silhouette of Taos pueblo against the sky, the color and light—all awakened in him an enduring excitement that sparked the founding of the Taos Society of Artists, which later took root in Santa Fe, too. These painters and sculptors, disenchanted with the frenetic pace "back East," were drawn to the West's freedom and openness and especially to Pueblo Indian culture, which they perceived as more "spiritual" than their own. Several had studied in Paris and there absorbed the current yen for exotic subject matter that had led Gauguin to the South Seas. These American artists returned to discover a profoundly exotic land in their own country—the Southwest. ✢

Opposite: The Callers by Walter Ufer, c. 1926. *National Museum of American Art/Art Resource*
Above: Artist Bert G. Phillips painting on location. *Kit Carson Historic Museums*
Left: Sangre de Cristo Mountains by Ernest L. Blumenschein, 1925. *The Anschutz Collection*

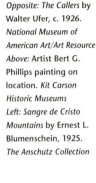

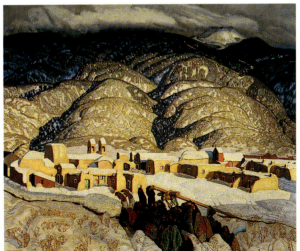

Georgia O'Keeffe: A Portrait with Apple Branch by Alfred Stieglitz, 1921. *Philadelphia Museum of Art. Right: Red Hills with the Pedernal, 1935. Museum of Fine Arts, Museum of New Mexico Opposite above: Another Church, Hernandez, New Mexico, 1931. The Anschutz Collection Opposite below: Kachina, 1931. The Gerald Peters Gallery, Santa Fe.* All paintings these pages © The Georgia O'Keeffe Foundation, Abiquiu, New Mexico

Of all the artists attracted to New Mexico, perhaps none has captured its stark beauty more vividly than Georgia O'Keeffe. Recognized as one of this century's foremost painters, O'Keeffe began her love affair with New Mexico in 1929, the year she arrived in Taos from New York to visit arts patron and socialite Mabel Dodge Luhan. From the first, she was captivated by the light, colors, and forms of the high desert country.

Already famed for her dramatic flower canvases and other works, O'Keeffe found fresh inspiration in New Mexico's canyon rocks, the bleached bones she found on long backcountry walks, and the sensuous forms of adobe

walls. At first she just visited in New Mexico, still living in New York with her husband, the photographer Alfred Stieglitz. Later she bought Rancho de los Burros, an adobe house that she furnished sparsely and opened up to the sky and cliffs with wide glass windows. In 1945, she bought an old hacienda in Abiquiu and moved there permanently after Stieglitz's death in 1946. O'Keeffe herself lived into her 98th year; working in the setting she found so endlessly inspiring, she never stopped breaking new ground in her acclaimed paintings and sculptures. ✧

"A RED HILL DOESN'T TOUCH EVERYONE'S HEART as it touches mine and I suppose there is no reason why it should…."

> *"One seems to have more sky than earth in one's world."*
>
> Georgia O'Keeffe

"TO ME THEY [BONES] ARE STRANGELY MORE LIVING THAN THE animals walking around.... The bones seem to cut sharply to the center of something that is keenly alive on the desert even tho' it is vast and empty and untouchable—and knows no kindness with all its beauty."

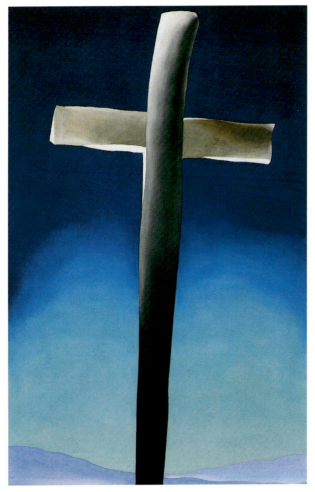

Gray Cross with Blue, 1929. O'Keeffe was fascinated by the rough crosses scattered through the lonely backcountry: they were made by the Penitentes—a religious sect. *The Albuquerque Museum. Photo Damian Andrus. Opposite: Ram's Head, White Hollyhock—Hills, 1935. Brooklyn Museum of Art, bequest of Edith and Milton Lowenthal.* "For me," O'Keeffe said, "painting the crosses was a way of painting the country."

Below: Mountain Spirit
Totem by Doug Coffin,
1981. Collection of
R. C. Gorman. Below right:
Early Morning in June by
Tom Noble, 1996. Cline
LewAllen Contemporary
Gallery

Few contemporary art scenes are as varied and lively as New Mexico's. It's estimated that out of a general population of 1.5 million, nearly 30,000 people living in New Mexico today identify themselves as artists. Both Santa Fe and Taos boast top-notch museums as well as legions of galleries and studios.

A long-standing tradition of fine arts, crafts, and architecture is today being enlarged by many cutting-edge artists. In painting, sculpture, and other media, artists from many backgrounds are turning to new forms to express both traditional and contemporary

The Sacred Taos Mountain #6 by Frank Romero, 1992. The ancient links between art and the land are forged anew in the works of contemporary New Mexican artists. *Courtesy of the artist*

ideas. In literature too, traditional concerns are being filtered through a new consciousness. Especially among Native American and Hispanic artists and writers, there is new freedom to experiment with old forms and subjects, and to incorporate "edgier" subject matter, such as political and social issues, into works of art and literature.

New Mexican artists continue to draw strength and inspiration from the land, but now they include urban landscapes as well as natural ones in their sphere of concern. ✦

The Lowriders by Meridel Rubenstein, 1981. Lowriders, most of whom come from New Mexico's Hispanic community, pride themselves on cars customized inside and out, down to every detail. *Brian Gross Fine Art*

Where Tradition Meets Innovation

Besides opening up to their physical surroundings, New Mexico artists are acknowledging, even celebrating the cultural transfer among Native American, Hispanic, and Anglo worlds. Architecture, too, has taken daring directions while continuing to refer to the traditional forms of local adobe structures. Unusual materials—straw bales, rammed earth, and even rubber tires—have also found their way into the contemporary architecture scene along with new interpretations of adobe.

In Santa Fe and Taos, cutting-edge art coexists with an abundance of traditional arts and crafts. In 1995, a huge event known as SITE Santa Fe took place during July through October. As many as 50,000 people flocked to this event, which featured installations, film and video, performance, painting, and sculpture by 31 artists, including Marina Abramovic, Jenny Holzer, Felix Gonzalez-Torrest, Swong Chi Tsend, and Andres Serrano. The event was held in a huge warehouse renovated by architect Richard Gluckman, designer of Pittsburgh's Andy Warhol Museum; the building continues to house exhibitions of new work and retrospectives of earlier artists.

Above: El Contrafuerte Grande de la Iglesia de San Ildefonso by H. Joe Waldrum, 1990. *Left: Near Los Ojos* by John Fincher, 1996. *Cline LewAllen Contemporary Gallery*

UFO Central

Something about New Mexico's wide-open skies and spaces must inspire UFO watchers; since the 1940s many sightings have been claimed, including a supposed crash-landing of an alien spacecraft near Roswell in 1947. The UFO Museum chronicles the entire history of this and other sightings and hosts an annual convention.

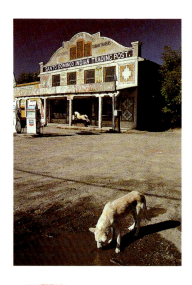

A Thirst for Shopping?

Located on tribal lands, the venerable Santo Domingo Trading Post is chock-a-block with imitation war bonnets and spears, authentic antique Navajo rugs, and everything in between. No tour of New Mexico would be quite complete without a visit.

Hand Me the Mail

Created by an anonymous artist, this intriguing and functional metal sculpture called the Hand Mailbox fronts a home on Santa Fe's Cerrillos Road.

Fresh Air and Fast Horses

Ruidoso, a mountain resort and the nation's capital of quarter-horse racing, also is home to this unique museum displaying Pony Express artifacts, photos, and fine art of the horse, including this life-size action figure.

Home Sweet Hacienda

Just outside Taos, the Martínez Hacienda was built in 1804 with fortresslike walls to guard against Comanche and Apache raids. Antonio Severino Martínez, a leading trader in the area, also turned his home into a showplace for the work of local builders and artisans; today weavers demonstrate spinning and working on looms in the old style.

A Whole Lot of Hot Air

Ballooning has thrived in New Mexico since the early 1970s; the Albuquerque International Balloon Fiesta, established in 1972, is among the world's largest balloon gatherings, attracting more than 500 colorful craft for 10 days each October.

Truth or Consequences

Named for Ralph Edwards's wildly popular radio and television show of the 1940s and 1950s, this town was originally a destination for health seekers looking to soak in its nearby hot springs, and was the title of a recent movie.

Place of the Pie

Near US 60 at the Continental Divide, Pie Town was first settled by a gas station owner who had a mining claim there. He built a roadside cafe for tourists; his advertisements for his pride and joy—pies—became the town's name.

Great People

A selective listing of native and adopted New Mexicans, concentrating on the arts.

Helen Cordero (1995–1994), Cochiti Pueblo potter, famous for storyteller figurines

Rudolpho A. Anaya (b. 1937), author of fiction, including *Bless Me* and *Heart of Aztlan,* about growing up Hispanic in New Mexico

Mary Austin (1868–1934), author and Indian advocate who settled in Santa Fe, best known for *The Land of Little Rain*

Ernest L. Blumenschein (1874–1960), co-founder of Taos Society of Artists; came to New Mexico in 1898 and stayed

William H. "Billy the Kid" Bonny, born Henry McCarty (1859–1881), the notorious outlaw; came to New Mexico as a boy

Christopher "Kit" Carson (1809–1868), legendary trapper, guide, scout, and Indian fighter, settled in Taos

Willa Cather (1873–1947), author, spent many years in Santa Fe; her novel *Death Comes for the Archbishop* set in New Mexico

John Denver (1943–1997), singer and songwriter, born in Roswell

Pete Domenici (b. 1932), U. S. senator of 1980s and '90s

Geronimo (1829?–1909), warrior of the Bedonkohe Apache and feared adversary of the U. S. army

Laura Gilpin (1891–1979), photographer who documented New Mexico people and landscapes for the WPA

Robert Goddard (1882–1945), physicist, rocket science pioneer; did much research in Roswell

Tony Hillerman (b. 1925), mystery novelist and essayist; eloquent spokesman for his adopted state

Conrad Nicholson Hilton (1887–1979), entrepreneur who built world's largest hotel chain

Paul Horgan (1903–1995), author and historian grew up in New Mexico; twice received Pulitzer Prize for his Southwest histories

Oliver LaFarge (1901–1963), author who settled in New Mexico; his novel *Laughing Boy.* won the 1930 Pulitzer Prize

Maria Antonita Martinez (1887–1980), San Ildefonso Pueblo potter famed for her "black-on-black" pottery

Joseph M. Montoya (1915–1978), New Mexico state representative, senator, lieutenant governor, and U. S. senator (1965–77)

John Nichols (b. 1940), author and essayist; noted for *The Milagro Beanfield War*

Georgia O'Keeffe (1887–1986), famed painter made New Mexico her home in the 1940s

Lewis (Lew) Wallace (1827–1905), Territorial governor of New Mexico (1878–81) and author of the novel *Ben-Hur*

Emmi Whitehorse (b. 1957), abstract painter of Navajo descent from Crownpoint

. . . and Great Places

Some interesting derivations of New Mexico place names.

Albuquerque   Founded in 1706 by Don Francisco Cuervo y Valdez, who named it in honor of the Duke of Albuquerque, viceroy of New Spain.

Angel's Peak   Mountains resemble a group of winged angels; they're part of the Garden of the Angels badlands area.

Bandelier National Monument   Given its English name for Adolph Bandelier, self-taught Swiss historian who came to study the New Mexican pueblos.

Cimarron   A river and a town; *cimarron* in Spanish means "wild" or "untamed," and the old cowhand town lived up to its name in the 1800s.

Clovis   Named for the French king by the romantic daughter of a Santa Fe Railway official. Prehistoric spearpoints found nearby also got the name.

Enchanted Mesa   The ancient Acoma people called this magnificent butte *katzino*—their word for "enchanted."

Las Vegas   The quiet New Mexico town, with its historic Victorian homes, couldn't be more different from its Nevada counterpart. The name means "the meadows."

Llano Estacado   New Mexicans still argue over the name of this endless arid plain. It might be from the literal Spanish, "stockaded plain" (did the distant mesas look like stockades?), or describe the yucca plants that rise like stakes in the flat land.

Loving   The town's third and present name is that of an early local cattle drover. The Goodnight–Loving Trail is a famed cattle trail.

Ojo Caliente   The town was named for the nearby hot mineral springs that have attracted visitors for centuries.

Rock Hound State Park   In this park near Deming, visiting "rock hounds" hunt for prized geodes.

Salem   First called Plaza by the Spanish, this town was renamed by a group of New Englanders, apparently homesick for their native Salem, Massachusetts.

Truth or Consequences   Named for the popular radio and television show of the 1940s and '50s, hosted by Ralph Edwards.

Valley of Fires Recreation Area   Near Carrizozo, this badlands area got its name from a Mescalero Apache account of ancient volcanic eruptions that created a "valley of fires."

Wagon Mound   Founded in 1850 by stockmen looking for pastureland, the town is named for a volcanic mesa that looks like a covered wagon—a landmark on the journey West.

Shiprock   A spectacular rock monolith known to the Navajo as Tse' Bit' a' i'—Winged Rock. To others it resembles a ghostly ship floating on the desert horizon.

NEW MEXICO BY THE SEASONS
A Perennial Calendar of Events and Festivals

*Here is a selective listing of events that take place each year in the months noted;
we suggest calling ahead to local chambers of commerce for dates and details.
Note: In nearly every month various Feast Days are held in many pueblos. For details,
consult the State Department of Tourism.*

January

At most pueblos
  New Year's Day Dances
  King's Day Celebrations
  Installation of newly elected
  governors, followed by dances.

Taos
  Taos Mountain Stampede
  Cross-country ski race.

Taos Pueblo
  Buffalo Dance

February

Angel Fire
  Angel Fire Winterfest
  World Shovel Race Championships
  Wacky downhill "skiing" event
  on shovels.

Dulce
  *Jicarilla Apache Centennial
  Celebration and Pow-wow*

Grants
  Mt. Taylor Winter Quadrathon
  Bicycling, running, cross-county
  skiing, and snowshoeing on
  75-km mountain course.

Picuris and San Felipe Pueblos
  Candelaria Day Dances

Valencia County Fairgrounds
  Baca Rodeo
  Southwest's largest rough
  stock rodeo.

March

At most pueblos
  *Spring Corn Dances; Easter
  celebrations (March/April)*

Albuquerque
  Fiery Food Show
  Annual trade show features
  chiles and chile products.

Deming
  Rockhound Roundup
  Rock and gemstone auctions;
  stone finishing.

Laguna Pueblo
  St. Joseph Feast Day

April

Alamogordo
  Trinity Site Tours
  Car tours of White Sands
  Missile Range atomic bomb site.

Albuquerque
  Gathering of Nations Pow-wow
  Arts and crafts, Native American
  dancers and singers from over
  700 Canadian and U.S. tribes.

May

At many pueblos
  Feast Days
  Corn dances, blessing of the
  fields, ceremonial races.

Albuquerque
  Albuquerque Festival of the Arts
  Two-week event celebrates per-
  forming, visual, and literary arts.

Silver City
  *New Mexico Square and Round
  Dance Festival*

Statewide
  Cinco de Mayo Spring Fiesta

Taos
  Taos Arts Festival
  Celebrates the visual, performing,
  and literary arts of Taos area.

Truth or Consequences
  Ralph Edwards Fiesta

June

Albuquerque
  New Mexico Arts and Crafts Fair
  Juried show, work by 200 artists.

Las Vegas
  Rails 'n' Trails Days
  Rodeo, art show, Tom Mix
  Film Festival.

Santa Fe
  Rodeo de Santa Fe

Silver City
  Tour of the Gila Bicycle Race

Taos
  Summer Chamber Music Festival
  Concerts, open rehearsals, and
  seminars, Taos School of Music.

July

Albuquerque
Native American Arts and Crafts Fair

Grants
Wild West Days
Carnival, parade, rodeos, etc.

Nambe Pueblo
Nambe Waterfall Ceremonial
Dances by many visiting tribes.

Roswell
UFO Festival

Santa Fe
Santa Fe Opera
World-class opera is performed in an outdoor amphitheater.

Santa Fe Stages
Presents international companies and its own productions June–August.

Santa Fe Chamber Music Festival
Six-week concert series.

Behind Adobe Walls House Tour

Spanish Market
Spanish arts and crafts displayed and sold.

Taos
Fiestas de Santiago y Santa Ana
Traditional festival in honor of the patron saint of Taos.

August

Deming
Great American Duck Race
Duck racing—for a $2,000 purse!

Farmington
Connie Mack World Series Baseball Tournament
Finals for amateur teams from the U.S. and Puerto Rico.

Gallup
Inter-tribal Indian Ceremonial
Fifty tribes gather for rodeo, parades, and other events.

Santa Fe
Indian Market
Largest U.S. show of Native American arts.

September

At many pueblos
Feast Days and Harvest Dances

Albuquerque
New Mexico State Fair

Gallup
Route 66 Bike Classic

Hatch
Hatch Chile Fiesta
At the "Chile Capital of the World," features crowning of Red and Green Chile Queens.

Santa Fe
Fiestas de Santa Fe
Nation's oldest community celebration, first held in 1712.

Taos
Taos Arts Festival
Two-week event features local artists' work.

October

Albuquerque
Kodak Albuquerque International Balloon Fiesta
600 balloons at one of the world's largest hot-air events.

Glencoe
Lincoln County Cowboy Symposium
Cowboy poets, musicians, chuck-wagon cooks, and artisans.

Las Cruces
Whole Enchilada Fiesta

Santa Fe
Santa Fe Furniture Expo
Nation's largest show of Southwestern furniture.

Shiprock
Shiprock Navajo Fair
Annual Northern Navajo Nation celebration.

Silver City
Cielo Encantado Kite Festival

November

Albuquerque
Southwest Arts Festival
Only juried national art event in New Mexico.

Socorro
Festival of the Cranes at Bosque del Apache National Wildlife Refuge

December

At most pueblos
Christmas Dances

Albuquerque
Christmas Eve Luminaria Tour
Millions of candles illuminate sidewalks, streets, and rooftops.

Santa Fe
Christmas at the Palace
Holiday activities held at the Palace of the Governors.

Statewide
Las Posadas
Reenactment of Nativity.

Zuni Pueblo
Shalako
Nightlong ritual reenactment of Zuni creation story.

WHERE TO GO
Museums, Attractions, Gardens, and Other Arts Resources

Call for seasons and hours when open.

Museums

ALBUQUERQUE MUSEUM
2000 Mountain NW, Albuquerque, 505-242-4600
Features permanent exhibits on the city's history and traveling exhibits of regional contemporary art.

BILLY THE KID MUSEUM
Fort Sumner, 505-355-2380
Exhibits of cowboy memorabilia, featuring those of the "Kid."

DEMING LUNA MIMBRES MUSEUM
301 South Silver, Deming, 505-546-2382
Frontier exhibits, Mimbres pottery, minerals and gems.

GEORGIA O'KEEFFE MUSEUM
217 Johnson St., Santa Fe, NM 87501, 505-995-0785
New museum houses a stunning permanent collection of the great artist's work.

HARWOOD FOUNDATION
238 Ledoux, Taos, 505-758-9825
Works by Taos artists, Native American arts and crafts, and a library are housed at the University of New Mexico.

INDIAN PUEBLO CULTURAL CENTER
2401 12th NW, Albuquerque, 505-843-7270
Showcases arts and crafts of New Mexico Pueblo culture.

INTERNATIONAL UFO MUSEUM AND RESEARCH CENTER
Roswell, 505-625-9465
Dedicated to study of UFO phenomena; features exhibits.

MAXWELL MUSEUM OF ANTHROPOLOGY
University of New Mexico, Albuquerque, 505-277-4404
Changing exhibits display artifacts of the Native American and Spanish cultures.

MILLICENT ROGERS MUSEUM
Four miles north of Taos on N.M. 522, 505-758-2462
Historic and contemporary art of the Southwest.

MUSEUM OF FINE ARTS
Lincoln and Palace, Santa Fe, 505-8270-4468
Handsome Pueblo Revival-style building houses contemporary Southwestern art and paintings by Taos School artists.

MUSEUM OF INDIAN ARTS AND CULTURE
708 Camino Lejo, Santa Fe, 505-827-6344
Traditional crafts of the Plains, Apache, and Navajo cultures.

MUSEUM OF INTERNATIONAL FOLK ART
706 Camino Lejo, Santa Fe, 505-827-6350
Stunning collection of folk art includes Spanish Colonial pieces plus examples from the world over.

NEW MEXICO MUSEUM OF NATURAL HISTORY AND SCIENCE
1801 Mountain NW, Albuquerque, 505-841-8837
Hands-on displays and innovative exhibits include an "active" volcano, and an elevator that takes visitors through time.

TINKERTOWN MUSEUM
121 Sandia Crest Rd., Sandia Peak, Albuquerque, 505-281-5233
A scale-model village created from a huge collection of miniature toys.

TURQUOISE MUSEUM
2107 Central NW, Albuquerque, 505-247-8650
Features gorgeous pieces from 60 mines throughout the world.

WHEELWRIGHT MUSEUM OF THE AMERICAN INDIAN
704 Camino Lejo, Santa Fe, 505-982-4636
A museum dedicated to the preservation of Southwestern Native American culture and ceremonial life.

Pueblos, Missions, and Churches

ACOMA PUEBLO
12.5 miles southwest of the junction of Routes I-40 and 23, 505-552-6604
Also called Sky City, Acoma is dramatically situated high atop a mesa. Continuously inhabited since the 12th century, it is also the site of the San Esteban del Rey Mission.

EL SANTUARIO DE CHIMAYO
Chimayo, 505-351-4889
This legendary shrine, with its sacred healing earth, hosts thousands of pilgrims every year during Holy Week.

ISLETA PUEBLO
Route I-25, 14 miles south of Albuquerque, 505-869-3111
Established in the early 13th century, it is the site of St. Augustine Church, one of the nation's oldest missions.

SAN FRANCISCO DE ASIS CHURCH
Ranchos de Taos, Route 68, 3 miles west of Taos, 505-758-2754
Built in the late 1700s, this splendid mission has been a favorite subject for many Taos artists.

SANTUARIO DE GUADALUPE
100 Guadalupe, Santa Fe, 505-988-2027
This 18th-century mission museum is the nation's oldest shrine to Our Lady of Guadalupe.

TAOS PUEBLO
Off Route 68, 2 miles north of Taos, Taos, 505-758-8626
This multistoried pueblo, continuously occupied since the 14th century, is the northernmost of New Mexico's 19 pueblos.

ZUNI PUEBLO
10 miles west of the junction of Routes 602 and 53, 505-782-5581
The largest New Mexican pueblo. Zuni craftspeople are renowned for their jewelry and fetishes.

Parks and Archaeological Sites

AZTEC RUINS NATIONAL MONUMENT
1.5 miles north of Aztec along U.S. 550, 505-334-6174
Pueblo ruins date from the 12th century; the site features a fully restored great kiva.

BANDELIER NATIONAL MONUMENT
Los Alamos, 505-672-3861
Dramatic ruins of 12th-century Indian cliff dwellings.

BOSQUE DEL APACHE NATIONAL WILDLIFE REFUGE
16 miles south of Socorro on I-25
This vast wetlands area is the destination of nearly 300 species of birds, including the rare and elegant whooping crane.

CARLSBAD CAVERNS NATIONAL PARK
27 miles south of Carlsbad on U.S. 62/180, 505-785-2232
One of the nation's most extensive cave systems features many subterranean rooms and rock formations.

CHACO CULTURE NATIONAL HISTORIC PARK
505-988-6727
Extensive and impressive ruins of 1,000-year-old pueblos and kivas, remnants of the Golden Age of the Anasazi civilization.

EL MORRO NATIONAL MONUMENT
Grants, 505-783-4226
Inscription Rock features ancient petroglyphs as well as inscriptions by passing Spanish explorers.

GILA CLIFF DWELLINGS NATIONAL MONUMENT
Silver City, 505-536-9344
Mogollon cave dwellings dating from the 13th century.

PECOS NATIONAL HISTORIC PARK
26 miles SE of Santa Fe via I-25, 505-757-6414
Features the 14th-century Pecos Pueblo as well as the ruins of a 17th-century mission church.

PETROGLYPH NATIONAL MONUMENT
6900 Unser Blvd, Albuquerque, 505-839-4429
Bears thousands of ancient rock art images and inscriptions.

WHITE SANDS NATIONAL MONUMENT
Alamogordo, 505-479-6124
The world's largest gypsum dunefield covers 230 square miles.

Attractions

AMERICAN INTERNATIONAL RATTLESNAKE MUSEUM
202 San Felipe, Albuquerque, 505-243-7255
World's largest collection of captive-born rattlesnakes.

ENCHANTED CIRCLE
*A scenic 86-mile loop heads out of Taos along the edge
of the Sangre de Cristo Mountains.*

LAS VEGAS
*This town, once a mercantile center on the Santa Fe Trail,
boasts more than 900 buildings on the National Register
of Historic Places.*

LINCOLN
*This historic town features 40 restored buildings from the
days of Billy the Kid and the Lincoln County Wars.*

OLD TOWN
Albuquerque
*Albuquerque's oldest district features an array of shops,
galleries, and restaurants.*

SANDIA PEAK TRAMWAY
Albuquerque, 505-242-9133
*The longest aerial tram in the country serves Sandia Peak
Ski Area and takes visitors to peak's summit.*

SPACE CENTER
Alamogordo, 800-545-4021
*This museum complex contains the International Space Hall
of Fame, as well as the Clyde W. Tombaugh Space Theater.*

VERY LARGE ARRAY
Plains of San Augustin, 20 miles west of Magdalena
*The world's largest radio-telescope array is composed of
27 dish-shaped antennas, each 82 feet in diameter.*

Homes and Gardens

D. H. LAWRENCE RANCH
Route 3, 15 miles north of Taos, Taos, 505-776-2245
*A gift to Lawrence and his wife from Taos arts patron
Mabel Dodge Luhan.*

EL RANCHO DE LAS GOLONDRINAS
334 Los Pinos Road, Santa Fe, 505-471-2261
*A living history museum, this restored Spanish colonial
settlement is the site of many events year-round.*

ERNEST L. BLUMENSCHEIN HOME
222 Ledoux, Taos, 505-758-0330
*The home of the renowned painter and Taos Society
of Artists co-founder is a perfect example of the
"Santa Fe style."*

KIT CARSON HOME AND MUSEUM
East Kit Carson Home via Route 64, Taos, 505-758-4741
Home of the frontiersman and famed explorer Kit Carson.

PALACE OF THE GOVERNORS
Santa Fe Plaza, Santa Fe, 505-827-6483
*The oldest public building in the nation, 200-year-old
structure was built by Spanish colonists.*

Other Resources

SANTA FE WELCOME CENTER
491 Old Santa Fe Trail, The Lamy Building, Santa Fe,
505-827-7336
*The center provides free information, maps, brochures, and
advice to visitors to New Mexico.*

STATE DEPARTMENT OF TOURISM
P.O. Box 2003, Santa Fe, 800-545-2040

STATE PARKS & RECREATION
408 Galisteo, Santa Fe, 505 -827-7465

CREDITS

The authors have made every effort to reach copyright holders of text and owners of illustrations, and wish to thank those individuals and institutions that permitted the reprinting of text or the reproduction of works from their collections. Those credits not listed in the captions are provided below. References are to page numbers; the designations *a*, *b*, and *c* indicate position of illustrations on pages.

Text

Harry N. Abrams: *Georgia O'Keeffe* by Charles Eldredge. Copyright © 1991 by Harry N. Abrams, Inc.

Chartwell Books, Inc: Recipe for "Black Bean Soup" adapted from *The Great Chili Pepper Book* by Gina Steer. Copyright © 1995 by Quintet Publishing Ltd.

Alfred A. Knopf, Inc.: *Death Comes for the Archbishop* by Willa Cather. Copyright 1927 by Willa Cather. Renewed © 1955 by the Executors of the Estate of Willa Cather. *Mornings in Mexico*, by D. H. Lawrence. Copyright 1927 by Alfred A. Knopf, Inc. By permission of Random House, Inc.

Ohio University Press/Swallow Press: *Masked Gods: Navaho and Pueblo Ceremonialism* by Frank Waters. Copyright © 1950 by Frank Waters. *People of the Valley* by Frank Waters. Copyright © 1941 by Frank Waters.

Penguin USA: Excerpt from the essay "New Mexico," from *Phoenix: The Posthumous Papers of D. H. Lawrence*, by D. H. Lawrence and edited by Edward D. MacDonald. Copyright 1936 by Frieda Lawrence. Renewed © 1964 by The Estate of the late Frieda Lawrence Ravagli. Used by permission of Viking Penguin, a division of Penguin Books USA Inc.

John Sedlar: Recipe for "Bizcochitos" adapted from *Modern Southwest Cuisine*. Copyright © 1986 by John Sedlar.

Simon & Schuster, Inc.: *The Land of Poco Tiempo*, by Charles Lummis. Copyright 1933 by Charles Lummis. (Charles Scribner's Sons, 1893)

Ten Speed Press: Recipe for "Green Chile Chutney," adapted from *The Great Chile Book*, by Mark Miller. Copyright © 1991 by Mark Miller. Reprinted with permission by Ten Speed Press, P.O. Box 7123, Berkeley, CA 94707.

University of Chicago Press: *Pueblo: Mountain, Village, Dance* by Vincent Scully. Copyright © 1989 by University of Chicago Press. Reprinted with permission.

University of New Mexico Press: *The House at Otowi Bridge: The Story of Edith Warner and Los Alamos* by Peggy Pond Church. Copyright © 1959 by New Mexico Press. *Edge of Taos Desert: An Escape to Reality* by Mabel Dodge Luhan. Copyright 1937 by Harcourt, Brace and Company. Renewed © 1965 by Antonio Luhan. Reprinted by permission of University of New Mexico Press.

Illustrations

THE ALBUQUERQUE MUSEUM: **59** Colcha. Wool on wool. 51 x 39¾"; **81** *Gray Cross with Blue*. Oil on canvas. 36 x 24". © The Georgia O'Keeffe Foundation; AMERICAN INDIAN CONTEMPORARY ART, SAN FRANCISCO: **1** *Hopi Snake Priest*. Beadwork on board. 12 x 12"; **67a** *Blue Night at Mount Taylor #600*. Mixed media on paper. 22½ x 30"; THE ANSCHUTZ COLLECTION: **9** *Chama Running Red*. Oil on canvas. 30¼ x 40¼"; **68** *Rodeo*. Oil on wood. 20 x 24"; **77b** *Sangre de Cristo Mountains*. Oil on canvas. 50¼ x 60"; **79a** *Another Church, Hernandez, New Mexico*. Oil on canvas. 10 x 24". © The Georgia O'Keeffe Foundation; APERTURE FOUNDATION, INC.: **24** *Church, Buttress, Ranchos de Taos, New Mexico*. © 1971 Paul Strand Archive; CRADOC BAGSHAW: **71b** Frank Waters; BOB BOZE BELL: **38a** Billy the Kid. Oil on canvas. 28 x 34"; BROOKLYN MUSEUM OF ART: **80** *Ram's Head, White Hollyhock—Hills*. Oil on canvas. 30 x 36". Bequest of Edith and Milton Lowenthal. 1992.11.28. © The Georgia O'Keeffe Foundation; DIANA BRYER: **47** *Making Chile Ristras*. Oil on linen. 30 x 40"; BURLINGTON NORTHERN SANTA FE RAILWAY COMPANY ART COLLECTION: **39** *The Old Santa Fe Trail*. Oil on canvas. 25 x 32"; CENTER FOR SOUTHWEST RESEARCH, UNIVERSITY OF NEW MEXICO: **40b** Boss Saloon. Neg. 000-179-0778; **41b** Cliff Mine. Neg. 000-119-0609; **71c** D. H. Lawrence. Neg. 986-010-0002; CLINE LEWALLEN CONTEMPORARY GALLERY: **27a** *31 • 12 • 82 #V*. Watercolor and ink. 30 x 22"; **82b** *Early Morning in June*. Watercolor and ink. 26 x 26"; **85b** *Near Los Ojos*. Oil on canvas. 36 x 48"; CRISTOF'S, SANTA FE: **11** Pictorial rug; DEWEY TRADING COMPANY: **46b** *Chile Blanket*. 64 x 64"; DIA CENTER FOR THE ARTS: **23** *The Lightning Field*; EITELJORG MUSEUM OF AMERICAN INDIANS AND WESTERN ART: **62** *The Plasterer*. Oil on canvas. 42 x 30"; FOODPIX: **60a, b**; GALLUP INTERTRIBAL INDIAN CEREMONIAL: **26b** Seed jar. 4¼ x 6"; R. C. GORMAN COLLECTION: **82a** *Mountain Spirit Totem*. Wood and acrylic. 6' x 4' x 24'; BRIAN GROSS FINE ART, SAN FRANCISCO: **84** *The*

Lowriders. Ektacolor print. 16 x 20"; THE HARMSEN COLLECTION, DENVER, COLORADO: **20** *The Ghost of Carlsbad Caverns.* Oil on canvas. 20 x 24"; HARWOOD MUSEUM OF THE UNIVERSITY OF NEW MEXICO: **48** *Decoration Day.* Tempera. 61 x 76 cm.; THE HEARD MUSEUM, PHOENIX: **65b** Storyteller figure. Clay, glaze, pigment. 11 x 5 x 8½"; **66b** *Ozone Madonna.* Painted mahogany and steel. 57 x 24 x 12"; **67b** *Navajo Woman.* Watercolor on paper. 73 x 58.5 cm.; DAVID G. HOUSER: **87a** Horse figure; KENNEDY GALLERIES, INC., NEW YORK: **70a** *The Marin House.* Watercolor and pencil. 10½ x 14½"; KIT CARSON HISTORIC MUSEUMS: **37** Kit Carson; **77a** Bert Phillips; ALFRED A. KNOPF, INC: **14b** Watercolor from *Trout* by James Prosek, © 1996; BONNIE KAMIN: **87c** Hacienda; HERB LOTZ: **14c** State Capitol; FRED LYON: **86c** Mailbox; NEDRA MATTEUCI'S FENN GALLERIES: **35** *The Sunset Dance.* Oil on canvas. 10 x 14"; MORNING STAR GALLERY: **40a** Zuni pin; TERRENCE MOORE: **54a** El Vado Motel; MUSEUM OF FINE ARTS, MUSEUM OF NEW MEXICO: **49** *Untitled* (Koshares). Watercolor. Gift of Mrs. Johnson McNutt; **75** *The Guitarist.* Oil on canvas. 35 x 32"; MUSEUM OF INTERNATIONAL FOLK ART, A UNIT OF THE MUSEUM OF NEW MEXICO: **2** *Tree of Life.* Carved cottonwood. 21 x 26". International Folk Art Foundation Collection; **58a** Chair. Carved pine. Museum of New Mexico Collections; **58b** Mirror. Tin with wallpaper. 22" h. International Folk Art Foundation Collection; MUSEUM OF NEW MEXICO: **17a** Willa Cather. Neg. 7112; **33** *Don Diego de Vargas.* Neg. 11409; **34b** Spur. Neg. 152510; **36** *View of Santa Fe Plaza.* Oil on canvas. 48 x 60"; **38b** Elfego Baca. Neg. 87485; **41a** *Santa Fe in the 1880s.* Oil on canvas. 26 x 32"; **72a** Playbill. Neg. 99827; **72b** Mary Austin, c. 1914. Neg. 45221; NATIONAL ARCHIVES: **32a** Map by Richard Kern; NATIONAL COWBOY HALL OF FAME AND WESTERN HERITAGE CENTER: **44-45** *An Afternoon of the Sheep Herder.* Oil on canvas. 28 x 50". Gift of J. Vernehawn; NATIONAL GEOGRAPHIC IMAGE COLLECTION: **12a** New Mexico flag, illustration by Marilyn Dye Smith; **12b** Yucca and roadrunner, illustration by Robert E. Hynes; NATIONAL MUSEUM OF AMERICAN ART/ART RESOURCE: **31b** *Elk-Foot of the Taos Tribe.* Oil on canvas. 78¼ x 36⅜". 1910.9.5; **50** *Corn Dance, Taos Pueblo.* Oil on canvas. 50¼ x 40¼"; **69b** *Vaquero.* Cast fiberglass and epoxy. 16½' h.; **76** *The Callers.* Oil on canvas. 50½ x 50½". Gift of Mr. and Mrs. R. Crosby Kemper, Jr.; NATURAL HISTORY MUSEUM OF LOS ANGELES COUNTY, SEAVER CENTER FOR WESTERN HISTORY: **34a** Saddle; NEW MEXICO

MUSEUM OF NATURAL HISTORY AND SCIENCE: **15c** Dinosaur; NEW YORK STATE MUSEUM: **14a** Anise (sweet cicely) from *Flora of the State of New York* by John Torrey, 1843; NIMAN FINE ART, SANTA FE: **66** *Maiden.* Bronze, edition of nine. 54 x 12 x 11"; HISTORIC OLD TOWN TURQUOISE MUSEUM, ALBUQUERQUE: **12c**; THE PARKS GALLERY, TAOS: **56a** *Angel Trestero.* Painted wood cabinet. 68" h.; THE GERALD PETERS GALLERY, SANTA FE: **22** *Storm.* Oil on canvas. 17 x 19½"; **79b** *Kachina.* Oil on panel. 20 x 16". © The Georgia O'Keeffe Foundation; PHILADELPHIA MUSEUM OF ART: **78a** *Georgia O'Keeffe: A Portrait with Apple Branch* by Alfred Stieglitz, 1921. Gelatin silver print. The Alfred Stieglitz Collection; PRIVATE COLLECTION: **78b** *Red Hills with the Pedernal.* Oil on linen. 19¾ x 29¾". © The Georgia O'Keeffe Foundation; RANCHO MILAGRO PRODUCTIONS: **70b** *Mabel Dodge Looking at the Sanchez Kid,* 1992. Oil on board; FRANK ROMERO: **83** *The Sacred Taos Mountain #6,* 1992. Oil on paper. 19 x 29"; ROSWELL MUSEUM AND ART CENTER: **19** *Landscape, New Mexico.* Oil on panel. 25½ x 2¾"; THE SAN ANTONIO ART LEAGUE: **42** *Taos Farmers.* Oil on canvas. 40 x 36"; SANTA FE OPERA: **74a**; SHELDON MEMORIAL ART GALLERY, UNIVERSITY OF NEBRASKA: **43** *Furrowed Fields.* Oil on canvas. 28 x 36". Howard S. Wilson Memorial Collection, gift of Mrs. Wilson; SYGMA: **86a** UFO kids. Photo T. Soqui; TRIBAL TREASURES, HOLBROOK, ARIZONA: **27b** Deer kachina. 12½" h.; UNIVERSITY ART MUSEUM, UNIVERSITY OF NEW MEXICO: **29** *Hedipa, A Navajo Woman.* Albumen silver print. Gift of Mrs. William S. Brewster; U.S.D.A FOREST SERVICE: **26a** Smokey Bear; H. JOE WALDRUM: **85a** *El Contrafuerte Grande de La Iglesia de San Ildefonso,* 1990. Oil on canvas. 54 x 54"; MICHAEL WALLIS: **15b** 1935 map; **54b** Decal

Acknowledgments

Walking Stick Press wishes to thank our project staff: Miriam Lewis, Joanna Lynch, Laurie Donaldson, Georgia Finnigan, Daniel Golden, Adam Ling, Catherine Scott, and Kina Sullivan.

For other assistance with *New Mexico,* we are especially grateful to: Laurel Anderson/Photosynthesis, Jennifer Dewey, Eduardo Fuss, Jerry Jacka, Lindsay Kefauver/Visual Resources, Art Olivas at the Palace of the Governors, Jack Parsons, Richard Pearce-Moses at the Heard Museum, Judith Sellars at the Museum of Fine Arts/Museum of New Mexico, and Stephen Trimble.